Ultimate
Space Atlas

MAPS · GAMES · ACTIVITIES
and more for hours of galactic fun!

CAROLYN DeCRISTOFANO

NATIONAL
GEOGRAPHIC

WASHINGTON, D.C.

TABLE OF CONTENTS

This atlas takes you on an imaginary journey through the universe. With its attractive, informative maps; amazing photographs; explanatory diagrams; and a bounty of information, you will discover cool things about space and the objects that move around in it. From our moon to worlds far beyond, it will be a journey of exciting discovery.

SKY-HIGH

INNER SOLAR SYSTEM

OBSERVING SPACE

OUTER SOLAR SYSTEM

OUR GALAXY AND BEYOND

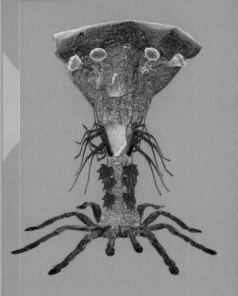

MAPPING SPACE

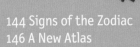

SPACE FUN

HOW TO USE THIS ATLAS

TOPIC IMAGE
An image behind the title sets the scene for the space objects studied.

Welcome aboard! This book is your vessel for a visual trip through the universe. For pre-trip orientation, these two pages highlight the features of this atlas. The design and elements of the articles are similar, and there is always a mix of images and information. Pages 6 to 33 introduce you to space, everyday astronomy, and maps of the night sky. Beyond that, travel through the universe wherever you wish. Follow Aunt Bertha's Important Safety Information and Space Travel Tips ... then strap yourself in for a wild ride far, far from Earth.

TITLE
This atlas is a collection of double-page spreads. Headings and subheadings provide a summary and flavor for each article.

INTRODUCTION
The main text is your gateway to the information on the spread. It might include general information, such as a space object's size, structure, atmosphere, and appearance, or any unique features or well-known examples.

SPACE TRAVEL ATTRACTIONS
Three major places of interest are listed and described here and usually appear on a map within the topic. (Throughout the introduction to space, pages 6 to 33, facts are listed under the title SPACE TRAVEL INFORMATION.)

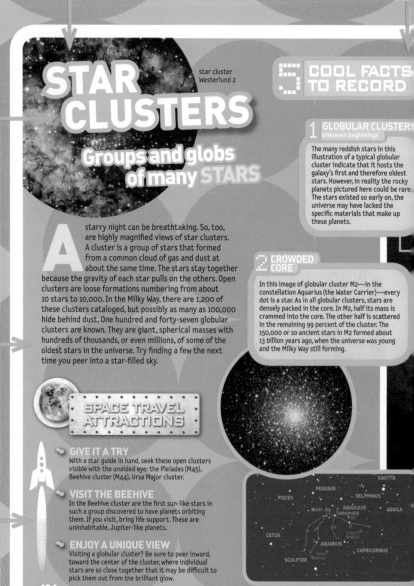

STAR CLUSTERS
Groups and globs of many STARS

star cluster Westerlund 2

5 COOL FACTS TO RECORD

1. GLOBULAR CLUSTERS
Unknown beginnings

The many reddish stars in this illustration of a typical globular cluster indicate that it hosts the galaxy's first and therefore oldest stars. However, in reality the rocky planets pictured here could be rare. The stars existed so early on, the universe may have lacked the specific materials that make up these planets.

A starry night can be breathtaking. So, too, are highly magnified views of star clusters. A cluster is a group of stars that formed from a common cloud of gas and dust at about the same time. The stars stay together because the gravity of each star pulls on the others. Open clusters are loose formations numbering from about 10 stars to 10,000. In the Milky Way, there are 1,200 of these clusters cataloged, but possibly as many as 100,000 hide behind dust. One hundred and forty-seven globular clusters are known. They are giant, spherical masses with hundreds of thousands, or even millions, of some of the oldest stars in the universe. Try finding a few the next time you peer into a star-filled sky.

2. CROWDED CORE

In this image of globular cluster M2—in the constellation Aquarius (the Water Carrier)—every dot is a star. As in all globular clusters, stars are densely packed in the core. In M2, half its mass is crammed into the core. The other half is scattered in the remaining 99 percent of the cluster. The 150,000 or so ancient stars in M2 formed about 13 billion years ago, when the universe was young and the Milky Way still forming.

SPACE TRAVEL ATTRACTIONS

GIVE IT A TRY
With a star guide in hand, seek these open clusters visible with the unaided eye: the Pleiades (M45), Beehive cluster (M44), Ursa Major cluster.

VISIT THE BEEHIVE
In the Beehive cluster are the first sun-like stars in such a group discovered to have planets orbiting them. If you visit, bring life support. These are uninhabitable, Jupiter-like planets.

ENJOY A UNIQUE VIEW
Visiting a globular cluster? Be sure to peer inward, toward the center of the cluster, where individual stars are so close together that it may be difficult to pick them out from the brilliant glow.

124

MAPS AND STAR CHARTS
To find many locations mentioned in the text, check out the sky charts and maps. Most of the maps are based on space telescope images. A bar scale compares the map size to real size.

5 COOL FACTS TO RECORD
These are five specific space objects, places to visit, or views to see in space. It is best to read them in order. Each accompanying story gives you expert knowledge about the item. Some text blocks have a pointer leading to the object, place, or view in an image, diagram, or on a map.

FUN FACTS
Did You Know? facts highlight unusual, unexpected, or interesting information about a topic.

MEASUREMENTS
In the text, measurements are given first in U.S. units then in metric units. The following abbreviations are used:
m = meters
km = kilometers
km/h = kilometers an hour
F = Fahrenheit, C = Celsius
t = metric ton

DID YOU KNOW?
Many of the star clusters have names beginning with M. The M means that they were listed in comet-hunter Charles Messier's catalog of nebulous objects. He kept a list to avoid mistaking them for comets.

OPEN CLUSTERS
M7, Scorpius constellation
An open star cluster called M7 shines in the constellation Scorpius (the Scorpion). About 1,000 light-years from Earth, it is one of about 1,200 open clusters in the Milky Way. M7 is known to backyard astronomers as a brilliant, large cluster in the night sky visible to the unaided eye.

DIGITAL TRAVELER!
Watch stars fling through space as part of a computer model showing a gas cloud becoming a star cluster. (3-D glasses optional.) Search the Internet for the phrase "Large Star Cluster Formation in 3-D by Matthew Bate."

an imaginary view from a planet's cave of the night sky with a neighboring planet and globular cluster

OUR GALAXY AND BEYOND

GALACTIC HALO
...ike bees swarming around hives, ...lobular clusters orbit around a spiral ...alaxy's center. While the galaxy's ...rms form a flattened disk shape, the ...rbits of these clusters occupy a ...pherical space around the bulge, ...art of a so-called galactic halo.

halo   globular clusters
arm

ORBITING CLUSTERS   galaxy center

GLOBULAR CLUSTER
M55, Sagittarius constellation
Light from a star on one side of the M55 cluster takes about 100 years to cross to the other side, and about 17,000 light-years to reach Earth. With binoculars, amateur astronomers enjoy its grainy, rather than cloudy, appearance, which hints at the 100,000 individual stars within.

125

DIGITAL OR TIME TRAVELER
This feature will suggest how you can discover even more about a space topic by thinking, investigating, and exploring on your own, often using a digital device.

CHAPTER TAB
To select a topic to explore or to keep track of where you are in space, look at the "tab" on the right-hand side of each article.

IMAGES
Space images in this book are a mix of photographs, telescope images, and artist's impressions of space scenes. Keep these image descriptions in mind:
Natural (or near natural) color: what you would see if you were observing the object with your own eyes.
Colorized: generally computer generated. Scientists choose colors to represent different temperatures, heights, energy levels, or other qualities.
Artist's impressions, artist's depictions, and illustrations: artists' visions of real-life events, processes, or objects often based on scientific facts. Where these are used, it is noted in the image caption or label.

DIAGRAMS
Labeled illustrations help explain scientific principles, ideas, and processes.

IMPORTANT! STAY SAFE!
Lots of times, Aunt Bertha's Travel Tips (or other parts of the book) suggest you go outside and take a look at things for yourself. It's a great idea, but to stay safe, see her tips on page 6.

SKY-HIGH

First steps to exploring SPACE

Chances are, your world hums with gadgets and media that grab your attention. But for a truly out-of-this-world experience, set all that aside and step outside. Fill your lungs with fresh air. Feel the warmth of the sun on your skin. Experience a sunrise or sunset. On a clear night, look up. In our sky, above the clouds and beyond are the distant objects of space. First, the sun, moon, planets, asteroids, meteors, and comets from our solar system. Then, faraway galaxies with their own stars and star systems. Each one calls us to take notice, to wonder, to explore.

AUNT BERTHA'S IMPORTANT SAFETY INFORMATION

Make sure a trustworthy adult provides permission, guidance, and company when you go outside or online.

For outdoor exploring at night, take a flashlight to help you find your way and to be seen. Avoid places where cars or other hazards are likely—keep to safe areas. Include something reflective on outer clothing. Dress for the weather.

One last, really important WARNING: Never look directly at the sun. Its dangerous radiation can damage your vision without you feeling a thing.

Aurora borealis, the northern lights, shine in the night sky at Abisko in the far north of Sweden. Seeing a clear, dark night sky from a remote location is a backyard astronomer's dream. Your sky may look different.

PROBING SPACE

Light, distance, and TIME

When you see an object, your eyes respond to energy coming from it: visible light in all colors of the rainbow. However, there are several kinds of light and our eyes cannot detect most of them. Each kind of light has a specific level of energy. Gamma rays and X-rays are high-energy light; ultraviolet, visible light, and infrared are medium energy; and microwaves and radio waves are low-energy light. Each astronomical telescope or detector collects a certain kind of light. Computers are used to translate the light into scientific images.

So where and what is "space" and how do we explore it? In astronomy, space begins high in Earth's atmosphere and may go on forever—or not. We may never know for sure. Space may seem almost empty yet within it are vast gas clouds, billions of stars with planets and rocks orbiting them, and a strange thing called dark matter. To observe and understand what's out there, astronomers use telescopes and other instruments to collect light that reaches us from space objects. From near or far, this light energy takes time to reach Earth. This atlas allows you to join scientists in their exploration and understanding of space.

5 COOL FACTS TO RECORD

1 DISTANCE AND TIME

Light from the moon takes little more than one second to reach Earth, so we see it nearly in real time. As distances reach trillions and more miles (km) away, light can take millions or billions of years to arrive. Because objects in space constantly change, by the time their light reaches us, they may have evolved into something very different from what we see.

DISTANCE AND TIME

Earth's moon	our sun	Jupiter
1.2 seconds ago	8.3 minutes ago	44 minutes ago

2 VERY SKY HIGH
Thermosphere and exosphere

Earth's atmosphere is made up of layers of air that block light from space. To get the best views, scientists send instruments such as the Hubble Space Telescope into orbit above the atmosphere. They are officially "in space" when they go beyond 62 miles (100 km) above Earth's surface.

3 MIDDLE ATMOSPHERE
Mesosphere

Here, between 30 and 50 miles (48 and 80 km) above Earth, there are no clouds, but the air creates friction. In this part of the atmosphere, any rock zooming in from space will heat up, glow, and burn as it rubs against the air—becoming a "shooting star."

4 LOWER ATMOSPHERE
Troposphere and stratosphere

Most weather happens close to the ground. Air currents, clouds, and light-scattering dust interfere with energy from space objects, so observatories—where telescopes are placed to view the sky—are often located atop mountains.

EARTH'S ATMOSPHERE

exosphere
6,200 miles
(9,977 km)

thermosphere
62–430 miles
(100–692 km)

mesosphere
50 miles (80 km)

stratosphere
30 miles (48 km)

troposphere
4–12 miles
(6–19 km)

space telescope—ultraclear images

Earth-based observatory—very clear images

amateur telescope—good images

5 SPACE TIME LINE

This diagram (not to scale) shows some specific space objects of increasing distance from Earth. Their light takes increasing time to reach us. The delay from Jupiter, for example— 44 minutes—may seem long, but that's practically nothing compared to the delay of the Pleiades star cluster. What you see today is what it looked like almost 50 years before the Pilgrims boarded the *Mayflower* for their journey to North America.

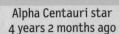

Alpha Centauri star
4 years 2 months ago

Pleiades constellation
444 years ago

Andromeda galaxy
2.5 million years ago

5 COOL FACTS TO RECORD

1 THE SUN'S LIGHT

We owe our familiar day-and-night cycle to the sun and one of Earth's key movements—its rotation. Earth spins around a central line, or axis, that runs from North Pole to South Pole, one turn about every 24 hours.

2 DAYTIME SKY

A complete day-night cycle follows this pattern: Sunrise marks when your part of Earth turns toward the sun; noon when it is facing the sun straight on; sunset when it turns away. Rain or shine, daytime Earth is always bathed in sunlight—even if clouds block much of the light from reaching us on the ground.

3 THE SKY AT NIGHT

Following sunset, your part of Earth is bathed in the planet's own shadow. Turned away from the brightness of the sun, on a clear night you can see other stars. How many you can see depends on the weather and, crucially, on how much light pollution may wash out your view.

northern winter
fewer daylight
hours

fall/spring

northern summer
more daylight
hours

axis line

southern summer
more daylight
hours

spring/fall

southern winter
fewer daylight
hours

4 THE TURNING SEASONS

As Earth orbits, or moves around the sun, it also tilts in space along its north-south axis. People who live north or south of the Equator notice changes not only in temperature but also in the length of daylight during each 24-hour day. The changes through the year mark the seasons: spring, summer, fall, winter.

DIGITAL TRAVELER!
For a simple animation and explanation of the seasons, solstices, and equinoxes, go to the website *pbslearningmedia .org*, search for "Summer and Winter Solstice: All About the Holidays," and select the video.

LIGHT AND DARK

Cycles of day, night, and SEASONS

Space constantly changes as planets, stars, moons, and other objects move. From Earth, the moon appears by day or night according to its own rhythm. Star patterns shift across the night sky. Sunshine hours increase and decrease through the year with the seasons. Daily, a brilliant sun rises, slides across the sky, then sinks below the landscape at sunset. On clear days, the sun shines in a sky that typically looks blue and empty. Why? As bright, intense sunlight beams through Earth's atmosphere, it brightens the whole sky, similar to car headlights shining into a foggy mist. This keeps you from seeing other space objects on the far side of the atmosphere.

full moon rising at night over a winter landscape in Alaska

SPACE TRAVEL INFORMATION

THE TERMINATOR
Look out for the terminator. It is the line that separates the bright, daytime side and the dark, nighttime side of the moon. It is an ever shifting boundary we see from Earth as the moon moves around our planet.

NO LUNAR DARK SIDE
There is no "dark side" of the moon, or side that is constantly in darkness. In fact, as the moon spins slowly, each part experiences day and night, each lasting about two weeks.

EQUAL DAY AND NIGHT
At the Equator, you'll get the same number of daytime and nighttime hours—almost exactly 12 for each. Also, sunrise and sunset happen very quickly here.

DID YOU KNOW?

If you watch sunrises and sunsets regularly, you will notice that for a time, the places on the horizon where the sun rises and sets seem to drift in one direction. Two days come each year when the direction of change stops—and then reverses. These times when the sun stops its drift are called the solstices. The midway points between these extremes are called the equinoxes.

PHASES OF THE MOON

The moon orbits Earth and is lit by the sun. As its position compared to Earth and the sun changes, we see different portions, or phases, of its illuminated face. Sometimes we see a full-on view—the full moon. Sometimes, as at the extremes of this diagram, it is just a sliver, called a crescent moon.

PHASES OF THE MOON—from left to right, then repeated

first quarter moon

full moon

third quarter moon

crescent moon

waxing (growing) moon

waning (shrinking) moon

crescent moon

THE TURNING SKY ABOVE

A constant movement of planets and STARS

The circular trails of starlight in the photo are created by the spinning of Earth.

Space is deeper than it seems to us as we gaze from Earth, with the stars overhead looking almost like they are projected onto a single, curved screen. In fact, stars exist at different distances from Earth. We use telescopes to look far into space and to create maps of the universe. Some of these maps are designed to show views of space from Earth. Others are created to show views as if you were looking back at Earth from a distant star or galaxy. Because Earth moves, our starry backdrop seems to shift around our world with the seasons. (See also pages 10 and 19.)

SPACE TRAVEL INFORMATION

WANDERING STARS
While stars seem locked into set positions, a few starlike objects move among them. Called "wanderers" by ancient Greeks, they turned out to be planets, other worlds like Earth, orbiting and lit by the sun.

SPIN SPEED
As Earth turns in its daily spin, it carries us with it. Your speed depends on where you are standing. For example, if you are on the Equator, where Earth is widest around, in one complete 24-hour spin you travel about 24,000 miles (38,620 km). That works out to 1,000 miles an hour (1,609 km/h). But you don't feel a thing.

FAST TRACK
Even without Earth's daily spin around its axis, you are on a speedy ride around the sun. In its orbit, Earth zooms through 66,600 miles (107,182 km) of space every hour.

5 COOL FACTS TO RECORD

1 THE ECLIPTIC
A line in the sky

The planets move around the sun in an almost level plane, as if spinning on a big, flat disk stretching out from it (see pages 32–33). With your eye at the disk's edge, this plane would look like a straight line. Any planets you see in the night sky appear just above or below the line, which is known as the ecliptic. Here, Saturn, Mars, and Jupiter are shown as they appeared along the ecliptic in a Northern Hemisphere summer sky in 2016.

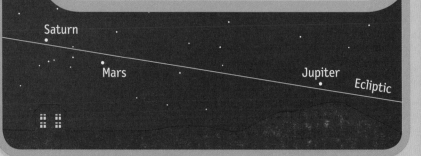

Saturn

Mars

Jupiter

Ecliptic

2 STARRY BACKGROUND

During Earth's orbit around the sun, its position in space constantly changes. The slight shift becomes clear by comparing the night sky of the same place at the same time on two separate evenings. In these illustrations, over a period of a month constellations Gemini and Orion move to the right and higher, and constellations Taurus and Lepus shift out of this framed view. Meanwhile, constellation Canis Major shifts into view. Eleven months later, the night sky will again look like the image on the left.

View from a Northern Hemisphere site at around 7 p.m. on a December evening.

View from the same site at 7 p.m., one month later.

3 CELESTIAL EQUATOR
North and south hemispheres

Like a giant Frisbee encircling Earth, an imaginary flat surface, or plane, extends straight out from Earth's Equator, into space. The line where its edge meets the sky—forming the celestial equator—divides it into northern and southern halves. This provides a useful reference for mapping objects in space.

4 THE CELESTIAL POLES
Aligning north and south

Like a slowly twirling umbrella held overhead, each of Earth's hemisphere's entire night sky seems to gradually circle around a central point. Polestars—the bright Polaris (North Star) and the quite dim Polaris Australis (southern polestar)—mark these points, which line up with Earth's North and South Poles.

5 SPINNING AND ORBITING

Like a top, Earth spins in space, each day completing one turn around its north-south centerline, or axis. This causes it to rotate toward, then away from, objects in space. That is why they seem to rise, then set. Earth also sweeps through space in its orbit around our sun, changing our seasons. This constant movement changes our viewpoint and our starlight scenery. (See also pages 18–27.)

CELESTIAL SPHERE

ECLIPSES— UNUSUAL VIEWS

When light from a star is BLOCKED

watching an eclipse through safety glasses

SIZE ILLUSION
The sun is about 400 times larger than the moon. Coincidentally, the moon is about 400 times closer to Earth. That is why the sun and moon look to us to be about the same size in the sky.

ONCE IN A WHILE
About once every 18 months, a total solar eclipse takes place somewhere on Earth. However, these eclipses aren't often seen at the same location. That happens only once every 375 years or so.

DON'T LOOK NOW
You can't see or feel sunburn-causing ultraviolet (UV) light but it constantly streams off the sun. Stay safe: View solar eclipses only through special glasses or telescopes with solar filters.

The motions of planets and moons can lead to events that can seem random, mysterious, or possibly terrifying to those who don't understand what is happening. For example, sometimes sunlight drains from the sky during the middle of the day, turning the moon blood red. Astronomers can explain these events with ease. Planets and moons glide through space, each moving along a regular orbit, or path. Sometimes—depending on where you're watching from—one will pass in front of another. If both objects appear to be the same size, the one closer to you will block the other, causing an eclipse. During a solar eclipse, the moon blocks the sun from Earth's view and sunlight from reaching Earth. Similarly, when the moon slips into the darkness of Earth's shadow, a lunar eclipse results. Depending on the type, an eclipse might last from about two to four hours, from start to end.

COOL FACTS TO RECORD

5

1 IN THE SHADOW OF THE MOON
Place your hand between a flashlight and a wall, and your hand's shadow makes a dark area on the wall. Similarly, a solar eclipse's daytime dimness is caused by the moon's shadow. Seen from space, the shadow forms a small circle that moves across the surface of Earth.

SOLAR ECLIPSE
The diagram shows the shadow of the moon on Earth during a solar eclipse. There is an inner shadow (black) and outer shadow (dark blue).

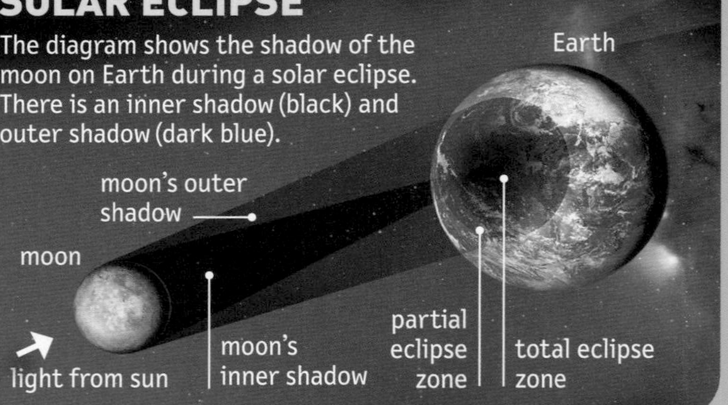

Earth

total eclipse zone

partial eclipse zone

moon's inner shadow

moon's outer shadow

moon

light from sun

TOTAL SOLAR ECLIPSE

A rare and awe-inspiring sight appears at the peak of a solar eclipse. At the moment when the moon completely covers the entire face of the sun, observers are treated to a view of wispy streamers of material that shoot out from the sun—the solar corona. Ordinarily, the sun's brilliant glow masks this detail.

PARTIAL COVERAGE
Moving circles

Not all eclipses are total. In a partial solar eclipse, only part of the sun will be blocked by the moon as we look from Earth. During a total eclipse, the maximum darkness can last as long as 7.5 minutes. As you might guess, the darkest time during a partial eclipse lasts less than this, and depends on how much of the sun is covered.

ECLIPSES ON OTHER PLANETS

Other planets in our solar system have moons, and they too can cast shadows when they block the sun's light. In our solar system, the shadows of Jupiter's 67 moons are frequently seen through Earth-based telescopes. In this colorized image, the three dark spots on Jupiter's surface are eclipses by the moons Io, Ganymede, and Callisto (see pages 74–75).

solar eclipse seen as the moon drifts in front of the sun

LUNAR ECLIPSE

When Earth's shadow falls on the moon, everyone on the night side of Earth witnesses a lunar eclipse—either as a nearly darkened moon or as a dimmed red disk. Seeing a lunar eclipse from the same location is not as rare as seeing a solar eclipse. Some years, people in a given place see up to three partial or total lunar eclipses.

DIGITAL TRAVELER!

Prepare to view the next eclipses to come your way by visiting the website *eclipse.gsfc.nasa.gov*. Find out when and where on Earth the next eclipses will take place.

OBSERVING SPACE

Finding our place in the UNIVERSE

The sky enchants us. There is much going on in the far reaches of space, above and beyond Earth. We know it as a place with depth and mystery, a grand collection of objects in an emptiness we can travel through. Like a great container, space holds our questions alongside real, physical objects—the familiar moon and sun, for example, along with planets and stars, stars, and more stars! In the last hundred years, scientists such as German-born Albert Einstein (1879–1955) have challenged our ideas of space, causing new excitement and new questions. There is so much beyond the reaches of our planet. Our exploration of space is just beginning.

AUNT BERTHA'S SPACE TRAVEL TIPS

Orient yourself with a compass. The compass needle points north, with south in the opposite direction. Take note of east—where the sun rises—and west—where the sun sets.

Stay alert to changes and patterns all around you—the position of the sun at sunrise, how your shadow changes over a day, what phase the moon is in.

If you peer into the night sky from a lit-up area, you will see only the brightest stars, but if you get out into the country, you'll see thousands of stars.

The Milky Way glows with the light of billions of stars.

PATTERNS IN THE SKY

Recognizing groups of bright STARS

5 COOL FACTS TO RECORD

L ook at a starry sky (or even a picture of one) and your mind probably begins to play connect-the-dots. Do you see squares, triangles, letters, creatures, other objects? The patterns you notice are likely the same star groups, or constellations, that have been recognized throughout history, across time and different cultures. In these similar patterns, different peoples have recognized different characters and objects related to their individual traditions.

1 INTO THE DEEP

Imagine being at the finish line on a 100-meter (109-yard) track, watching runners come toward you. In their lanes, the runners are lined up closely left to right, but their distances from you and from each other vary widely. Similarly, stars in a constellation seem connected left to right and up and down in the sky, but in depth they can be close or far from one another and from Earth. For example, in the Big Dipper, star Dubhe is more than 1.5 times the distance from Earth as Mizar.

SPACE TRAVEL INFORMATION

DIPPING INTO THE NIGHT SKY
Use the diagrams and maps on this page to find the Big Dipper. It's a star pattern that is part of a bigger pattern, the constellation Ursa Major, or Great Bear.

TIME AND LOCATION MATTER
The star maps opposite and on pages 20 to 27 show specific examples of what can be seen in the night sky at particular times and locations on Earth. What you see will vary depending on where you are, when you look, and how clear the night sky is at the time.

WHAT'S IN A NAME
As you stargaze, you might begin simply by looking for any star groups and patterns you notice. Once familiar with what you see, turn to this atlas to learn some "official" constellations. For scientists, agreeing on official groups and constellation names is like using a dictionary. It helps avoid mistakes and confusion.

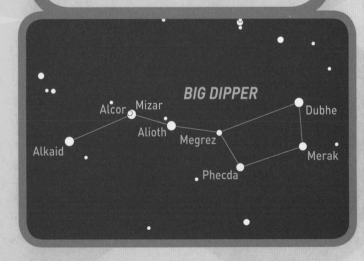

BIG DIPPER

Alcor Mizar
Alioth
Alkaid Megrez Dubhe
Phecda Merak

2 THE CELESTIAL SPHERE
Points of view

This diagram of Earth and its night sky can help us picture Earth floating in space. Constellations seem painted on a clear, spherical shell, called the celestial sphere. From Earth our view is that of a chick inside the shell, looking outward. What we see from our viewpoint is a reverse image of the star patterns as shown here, from the outside looking in. (See page 13.)

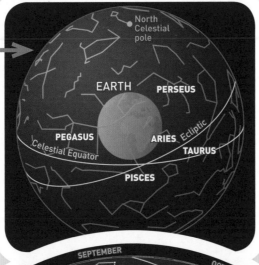

North Celestial pole

EARTH

PERSEUS

PEGASUS

Celestial Equator

ARIES Ecliptic

TAURUS

PISCES

3 THE ECLIPTIC
The sun's path

Compared to landmarks and background stars, the sun's point of rising seems to constantly change. The yellow line in the star map traces the path of this changing position. The path is called the ecliptic. Earth's orbit and its tilt on its axis create the sun's apparent change in position. Looking at the sky and the celestial sphere, we can watch the sun rise day after day across the ecliptic.

OBSERVING SPACE

SKY MAPS

The maps on pages 20 to 23 are sections of this flattened, circular view of the northern half of the celestial sphere; those on pages 24 to 27 are sections of a similar flattened view—of the southern half of the celestial sphere.

4 SKY MAPS
Flattened view

Maps such as this one show a view of the sky different from what a celestial sphere diagram shows. This is the view looking straight up at the night sky. Imagine making it by cutting off the top of the celestial sphere, pressing this half flat, and then looking from the inside.

KEY TO CONSTELLATION MAPS

- ••••• star magnitude
- • • variable star
- ○ open star cluster
- ⊕ globular star cluster
- ∘ galaxy
- ◦ planetary nebula
- □ other nebula
- ✦ supernova remnant

5 STAR MAP LEGENDS

The constellation maps on pages 20 to 27 show star magnitude—the larger the dot on the map the brighter the star appears to us from Earth. The maps also highlight other space objects you can see. To find out more about these, read pages 114 to 126 or see the glossary.

19

NORTHERN SKY

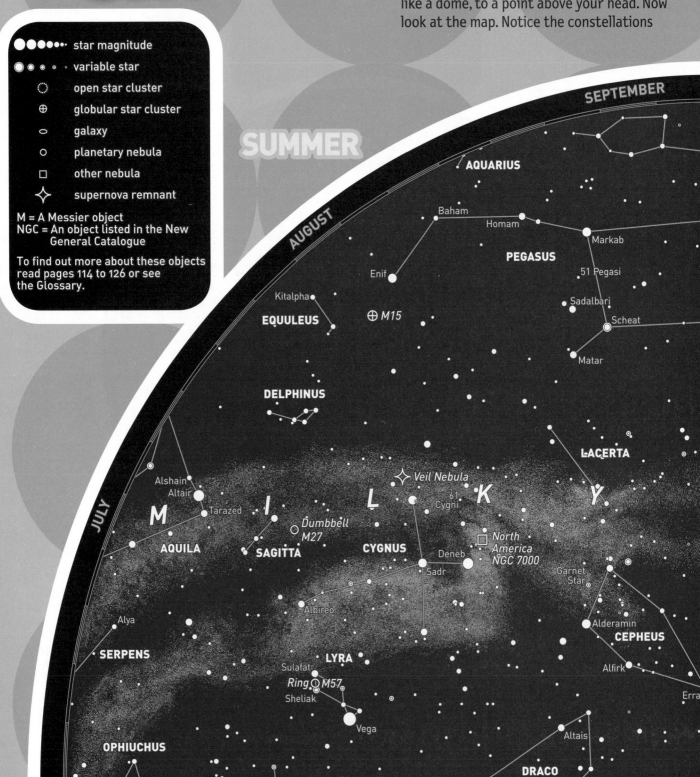

Before using maps like this summer map of the northern sky, orient yourself in 3-D space. At sunset, go outside (or imagine being there). Gaze eastward, your back to the setting sun in the west. North is left; south, right; and the ground encircles you. From all directions the sky arcs up from the horizon like a dome, to a point above your head. Now look at the map. Notice the constellations

- ●●●●●• star magnitude
- ●● ● ∘ · variable star
- ⊙ open star cluster
- ⊕ globular star cluster
- ⊘ galaxy
- ○ planetary nebula
- □ other nebula
- ✧ supernova remnant

M = A Messier object
NGC = An object listed in the New General Catalogue

To find out more about these objects read pages 114 to 126 or see the Glossary.

SEPTEMBER

SUMMER

AUGUST

JULY

AQUARIUS

Baham

Homam

Markab

PEGASUS

51 Pegasi

Sadalbari

Scheat

Enif

Kitalpha

⊕ M15

EQUULEUS

Matar

DELPHINUS

LACERTA

✧ Veil Nebula

Alshain
Altair

61 Cygni

K

Tarazed

M

I

L

Y

AQUILA

SAGITTA

⊘ Dumbbell M27

CYGNUS

Deneb

□ North America NGC 7000

Garnet Star

Sadr

Albireo

Alderamin

Alya

CEPHEUS

SERPENS

LYRA

Alfirk

Sulafat

Ring ○ M57

Errai

Sheliak

Vega

Altais

OPHIUCHUS

DRACO

along the semicircle's outer edge, and the month labels along the outer band: July, August, September, October, November, December. During a given month, the constellation near its label will rise during sunset. For example, at sunset in July, Aquila (the Eagle) is rising; at sunset in December, Orion (the Hunter) rises. This works for any map on pages 20–27. Wherever you are, you can figure out which constellation will rise at sunset any time of the year.

SPACE TRAVEL ATTRACTIONS

WATCH FOR CHANGES
Once a week, track constellations rising at sunset or early evening. Follow the changes along the edge of the circle on the map for your season and hemisphere.

THE QUEEN IN WHITE
Use the maps to identify the constellations found in the whitish, glowing band of the Milky Way. For example, see if you can find Cassiopeia (the Queen).

FIND THE NORTH STAR
Find Polaris on the map. If you are in the Northern Hemisphere, see if you can find it in your sky. How high up is it? The closer you live to Earth's Equator, the lower it will be. The closer to the North Pole you live, the higher it will be.

Each hemisphere's four wedge-shaped maps work together as one circle. The center point is directly overhead for someone standing at the pole (North or South). Off the pole, you'll see some stars and constellations that are not on this map. Exactly what you'll see depends on how far from the pole you are.

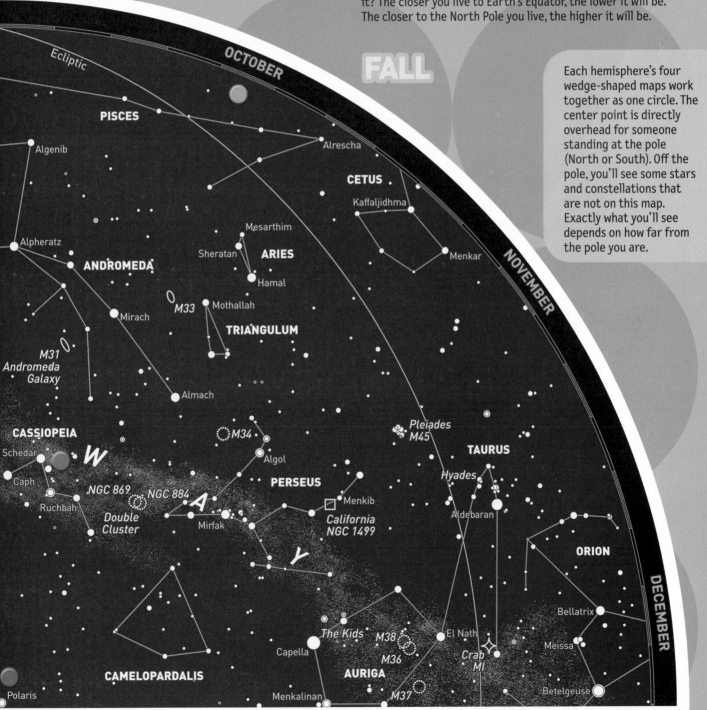

FALL

21

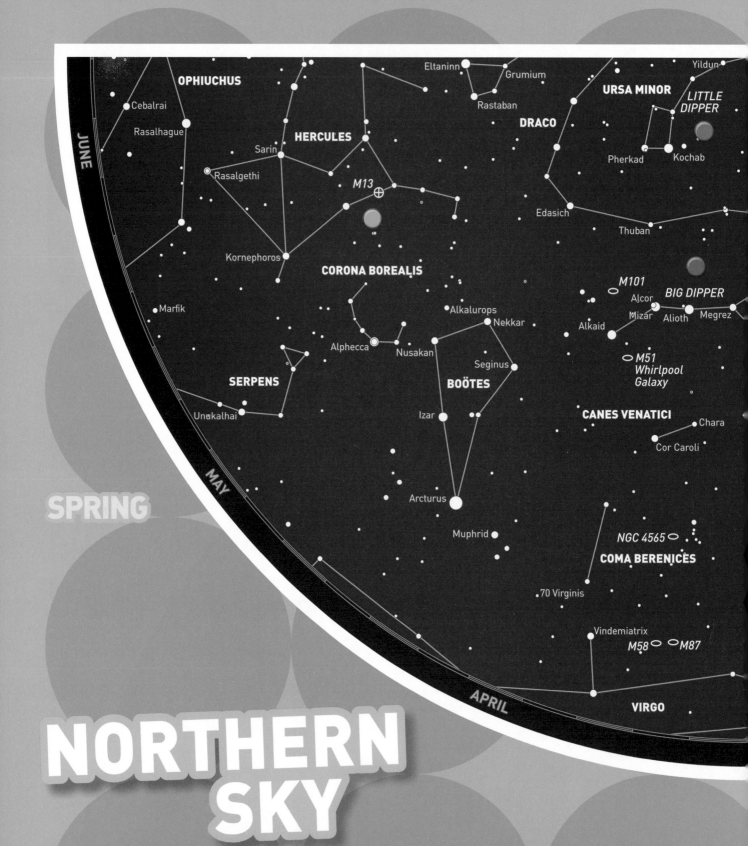

OPHIUCHUS

Cebalrai

Rasalhague

Eltaninn   Grumium   Yildun

Rastaban

URSA MINOR   LITTLE DIPPER

DRACO

HERCULES

Sarin

Rasalgethi

M13 ⊕

Pherkad   Kochab

Edasich

Thuban

Kornephoros

CORONA BOREALIS

M101

Alcor   BIG DIPPER

Marfik

Alkalurops   Nekkar

Mizar   Alioth   Megrez

Alkaid

Alphecca   Nusakan

Seginus

M51 Whirlpool Galaxy

SERPENS

BOÖTES

CANES VENATICI

Chara

Unukalhai

Izar

Cor Caroli

JUNE

MAY

SPRING

Arcturus

Muphrid

NGC 4565

COMA BERENICES

70 Virginis

Vindemiatrix

M58   M87

APRIL

VIRGO

NORTHERN SKY

Before using the sky maps on these pages, review how to orient yourself to your landscape (see pages 20–21). Once you are ready to use the northern winter and spring maps, notice that the months of the year shown along the outer edge run clockwise from January through June, beginning near the upper right corner of page 23. As with all sky maps (pages 20–27), the constellation near each month's label will be rising at sunset during that month. For example, expect to see Hydra (the Water Serpent) rising as the sun sets in February. Once you find the rising constellation, use it as a reference point. For instance, from Hydra, look north and higher in the sky to locate Leo (the Lion).

Menkalinan
AURIGA
M35
ORION
Propus
Tejat
Mebsuta
Alhena
Rosette NGC 2237
M81
Muscida
LYNX
GEMINI
Mekbuda
Castor
Wasat
Dubhe
Talitha
Pollux
Gomeisa
Merak
CANIS MINOR
Owl M97
Phecda
Procyon
URSA MAJOR
Tania Borealis
JANUARY
Tania Australis
Asellus Borealis
Praesepe M44
47 Ursae Majoris
Asellus Australis
CANCER
LEO MINOR
Rasalas
Alterf
HYDRA
Acubens
Alula Borealis
Adhafera
Alula Australis
Algieba
WINTER
Zosma
LEO
Regulus
Chort
M96
Denebola
M66
Zavijava
FEBRUARY
Ecliptic
MARCH

Try using the maps to hop from one constellation to another. For example, in February or March, notice Leo (the Lion) rising. A bit higher in the sky, can you find Ursa Major (the Great Bear)? Can you locate Lynx?

SPACE TRAVEL ATTRACTIONS

M13 GLOBULAR CLUSTER
This deep space mass of stars lies in the constellation Hercules, which can be seen throughout the summer months high overhead in the Northern Hemisphere.

TOO MUCH LIGHT TO SEE
Find the Little Dipper—then count how many of the four stars in the nearly rectangular bowl you can see. This can point out how much artificial lighting washes out your sky: The fewer you see, the greater the washout effect.

TELLING TIME WITH THE BIG DIPPER
Once a week for several months, look at the Big Dipper. A few times a night, note where the handle points and soon you'll notice a pattern. You can use the handle's position to tell time.

●●●●●•• star magnitude
⊙ galaxy
◎ ◉ ⊙ • variable star
○ planetary nebula
open star cluster
□ other nebula
⊕ globular star cluster
✦ supernova remnant

M = A Messier object
NGC = An object listed in the New General Catalogue

To find out more about these objects read pages 114 to 126 or see the Glossary.

23

SOUTHERN SKY

T hroughout history, peoples living in the Southern Hemisphere have always been familiar with the stars in their sky. They named the star patterns they saw. When northern explorers came south of the Equator, they renamed the constellations based on their own cultures. They also continued to place south at the bottom of their maps. This is why the Southern Hemisphere

●●●●●·· star magnitude
●●· · variable star
○ open star cluster
⊕ globular star cluster
⊙ galaxy
○ planetary nebula
□ other nebula
✧ supernova remnant

M = A Messier object
NGC = An object listed in the New General Catalogue

To find out more about these objects read pages 114 to 126 or see the Glossary.

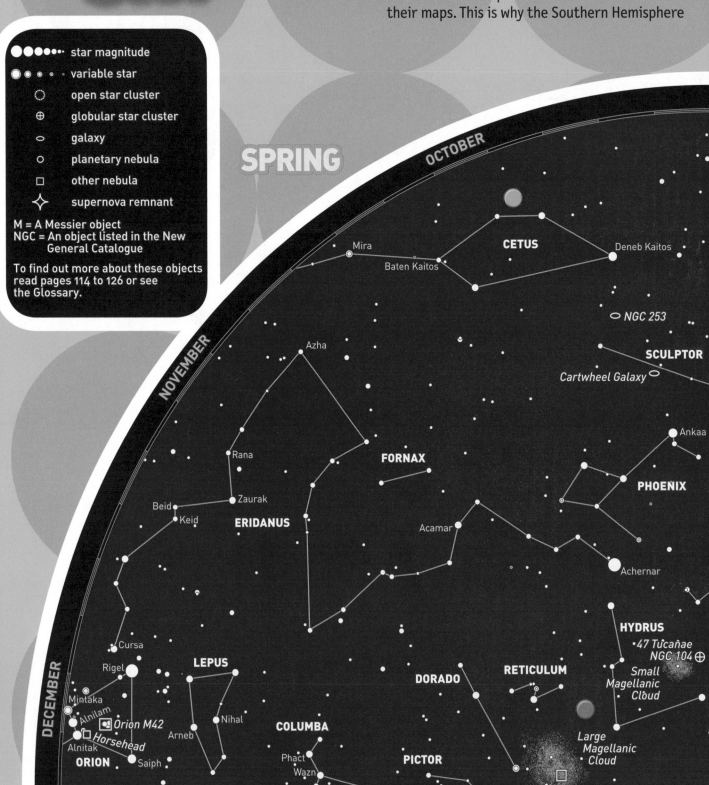

SPRING

OCTOBER

Mira
Baten Kaitos
CETUS
Deneb Kaitos

NGC 253
SCULPTOR
Cartwheel Galaxy

NOVEMBER

Azha

Ankaa

FORNAX

PHOENIX

Rana

Acamar

Beid
Keid
ERIDANUS

Achernar

Zaurak

HYDRUS

DECEMBER

Cursa

• 47 Tucañae
NGC 104 ⊕

Rigel
LEPUS

Small Magellanic Cloud

DORADO
RETICULUM

Mintaka
Alnilam
Orion M42
Nihal

Alnitak
Horsehead
Arneb
COLUMBA

Large Magellanic Cloud

ORION
Saiph

Phact
Wazn
PICTOR

sky maps represent the bottom half of the celestial sphere shown on page 19. The map here and on pages 26–27 show the sky dome as seen by someone on the South Pole, looking directly overhead, with the dome carefully flattened into a circle. For general tips on how to the read the maps, see pages 20–23.

SPACE TRAVEL ATTRACTIONS

OCTOBER'S RISING WHALE
After getting your bearings outdoors—north, south, east, west—look opposite the setting sun for a rising constellation. It should match the one on the map shown closest to the current month. For example, in October in the south look for Cetus (the Whale) rising at dusk.

SOUTHERN SPECIALS
Seek out the Large and Small Magellanic Clouds. These two patches of light are galaxies—masses of stars and gas—that are thought to orbit our own galaxy, the Milky Way (see pages 104–105 and 126–127).

APPEARING EVERYWHERE
Some constellations are visible from both hemispheres. See if you can find some of these examples in the "overlapping" northern and southern skies: Aquila (the Eagle), Serpens (the Snake), Orion (the Hunter).

Get used to some north-south differences as you look at these maps. Here, in the southern sky, the months on the star maps run counterclockwise—from July in the lower right of the southern winter map to December in the southern spring map. When it is spring in the Southern Hemisphere, it is fall in the Northern Hemisphere.

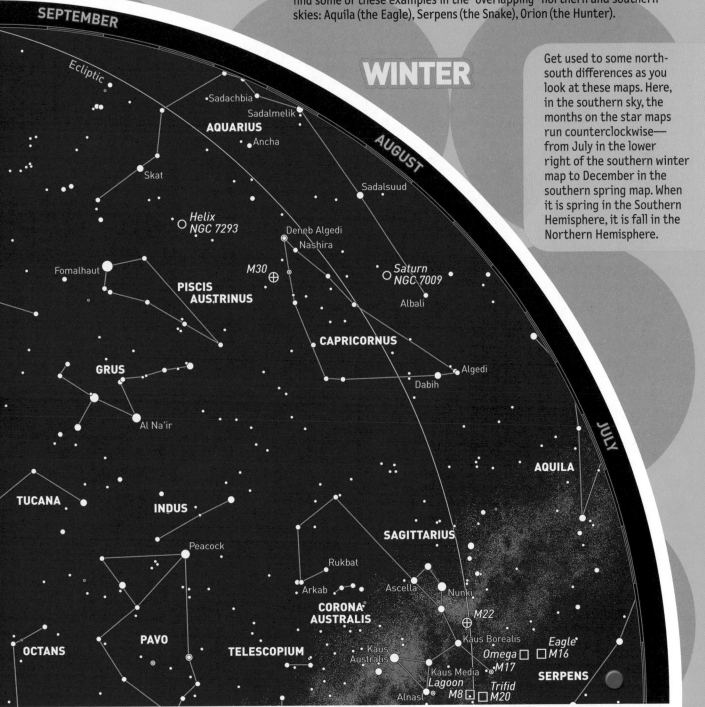

SEPTEMBER

WINTER

AUGUST

JULY

Ecliptic

Sadachbia
Sadalmelik
AQUARIUS
Ancha
Skat

Helix
NGC 7293

Deneb Algedi
Nashira

Sadalsuud

M30 ⊕

Saturn
NGC 7009
Albali

Fomalhaut

PISCIS
AUSTRINUS

CAPRICORNUS

GRUS

Algedi
Dabih

Al Na'ir

AQUILA

TUCANA

INDUS

Peacock

SAGITTARIUS

Rukbat

Arkab

Ascella

Nunki

CORONA
AUSTRALIS

⊕ M22

Eagle
□ M16

OCTANS

PAVO

TELESCOPIUM

Kaus
Australis

Kaus Borealis

Omega □
□ M17

SERPENS

Kaus Media

Lagoon

Alnasl

M8 □ □ M20

Trifid

COLUMBA

PICTOR

Furud

Canopus

VOLANS

Mirzam

CHAMAELEON

CANIS MAJOR

CARINA

Miaplacidus

Sirius

Adhara

Avior

Wezen

Aspidiske

IC 2602

Aludra

PUPPIS

Regor

MONOCEROS

Naos

M I L K Y

*Eta
Carinae
NGC 3372

Suhail

VELA

Gacrux

JANUARY

PYXIS

M48

SUMMER

Alphard

HYDRA

Alkes

FEBRUARY

CRATER

SEXTANS

MARCH

SOUTHERN SKY

T he Milky Way glows with stunning brightness in the Southern Hemisphere, where there is less light pollution than in the Northern Hemisphere to wash out the great views. In the southern sky, several unique features stand out, such as the Coalsack Nebula (in the region of the star Acrux), the Large and Small Magellanic Clouds, and the closest star to our sun, Alpha Centauri. These alone make it worth the effort of learning the sky map. Also in the Southern Hemisphere the moon appears upside down, as if the view of it from the northern sky was looked at in a mirror.

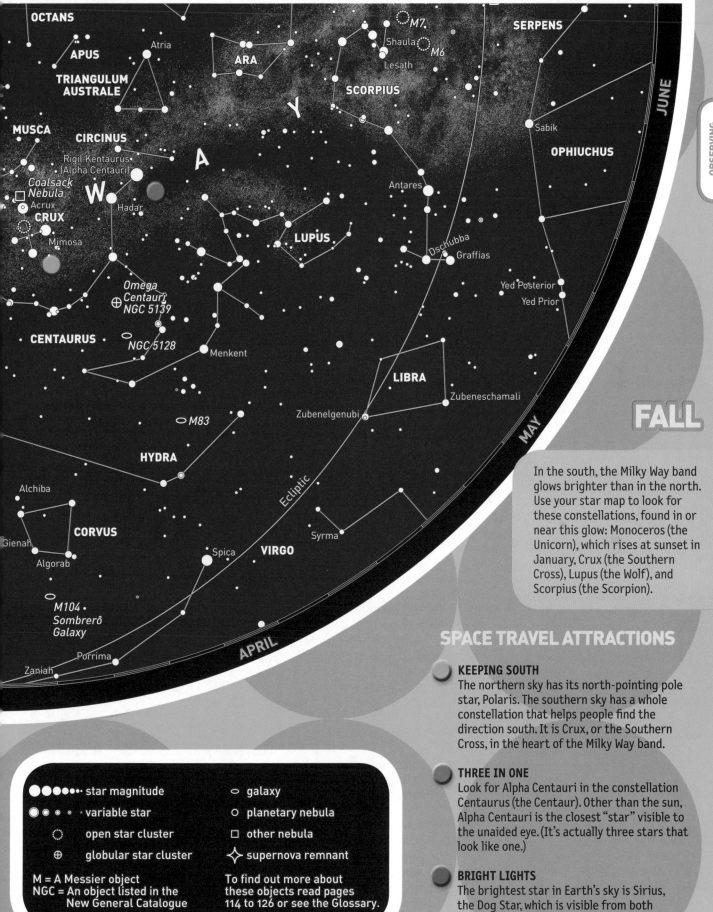

OCTANS

APUS
Atria

TRIANGULUM
AUSTRALE

ARA

M7
Shaula
Lesath
M6

SERPENS

SCORPIUS

JUNE

MUSCA

CIRCINUS

Sabik

OPHIUCHUS

Rigil Kentaurus
(Alpha Centauri)

Coalsack
Nebula
Acrux

CRUX

Mimosa

Hadar

W

A

Y

Antares

LUPUS

Dschubba
Graffias

Yed Posterior
Yed Prior

Omega
Centauri
NGC 5139

CENTAURUS

NGC 5128

Menkent

LIBRA

Zubeneschamali

M83

Zubenelgenubi

HYDRA

FALL

Ecliptic

MAY

Alchiba

CORVUS

Gienah

Algorab

Syrma

Spica

VIRGO

M104
Sombrero
Galaxy

Porrima

APRIL

Zaniah

In the south, the Milky Way band glows brighter than in the north. Use your star map to look for these constellations, found in or near this glow: Monoceros (the Unicorn), which rises at sunset in January, Crux (the Southern Cross), Lupus (the Wolf), and Scorpius (the Scorpion).

SPACE TRAVEL ATTRACTIONS

KEEPING SOUTH
The northern sky has its north-pointing pole star, Polaris. The southern sky has a whole constellation that helps people find the direction south. It is Crux, or the Southern Cross, in the heart of the Milky Way band.

THREE IN ONE
Look for Alpha Centauri in the constellation Centaurus (the Centaur). Other than the sun, Alpha Centauri is the closest "star" visible to the unaided eye. (It's actually three stars that look like one.)

BRIGHT LIGHTS
The brightest star in Earth's sky is Sirius, the Dog Star, which is visible from both hemispheres, in the constellation Canis Major (the Great Dog).

●●●●●●· star magnitude   ○ galaxy

◎◎◎ ◌ · variable star   ○ planetary nebula

◌ open star cluster   □ other nebula

⊕ globular star cluster   ✧ supernova remnant

M = A Messier object
NGC = An object listed in the
New General Catalogue

To find out more about these objects read pages 114 to 126 or see the Glossary.

FAR-FLUNG UNIVERSE
Steps through SPACE

Modern astronomers have access to lots of technology that helps them explore the universe—powerful telescopes, remote-controlled spacecraft, landers, rovers, and specialized detectors. Scientists also find new, creative ways to interpret all the information these technologies gather from space. With these tools, they have discovered an order, a repetitive pattern of structure, to our universe. As far as we can see, matter—the material stuff that every object is made of—is not randomly scattered in space but is gathered in big clumps. Like a small gift inside a series of bigger and bigger gift packages, our planet Earth is nestled within this structure—as is every other planet orbiting its own star.

5 COOL FACTS TO RECORD

2 STELLAR NEIGHBORS
Near yet far

Stars neighbor other stars. Each may be the center of its own planetary system. The closest neighbor to the sun, our own star, is Proxima Centauri, seen in this Hubble Space Telescope image. Proxima Centauri is also known as Alpha Centauri C and is part of a three-star system along with Alpha Centauri A and Alpha Centauri B. With unaided eyes, we see them as one bright star in the sky.

1 OUR SOLAR SYSTEM
Home territory

The pulling force of gravity is a grand organizer of our solar system, shown here as a diagram. Gravity keeps our planets revolving around our central, spinning sun. It pulls planets toward one another, and it keeps moons around planets. Gravity is an important force throughout the universe.

3 MILKY WAY
Our galaxy

Our solar system and its neighboring stars are about two-thirds of the way out from the center of the Milky Way galaxy—a vast community of stars, all bound together by gravity. Just as moons rotate around a planet and a planet around its central star, the billions of stars in our Milky Way also rotate around the galactic center. Near the edge of the Milky Way, our solar system's rotation takes about 230 million years to complete. Scientists estimate there are about 100 billion galaxies in the universe.

an artist's impression of the Milky Way

4 LOCAL GALACTIC GROUP
Community of galaxies

Just as a set of stars might be found together, neighboring galaxies also form groups. M31, the Andromeda galaxy, seen in this Earth-based telescope image, is one of the Milky Way's close neighbors. The two galaxies are part of the Local Group, which includes about 30 galaxies. Pulled toward each other by gravity, galaxies sometimes merge over millions of years (see pages 128–129).

5 GALACTIC CLUSTERS
Deep space

Far out in the universe, groups of galaxies form clusters, like this one. Almost every object in this photograph is a galaxy, each with its own billions of stars, and each star with its own possible solar system. The universe is huge for sure.

OUR SOLAR SYSTEM
Objects orbiting the SUN

SOLAR SYSTEM DATA

Diameter: about nine million million miles (14.5 million million km)

Farthest point visited by people: 239,000 miles (384,635 km), the moon

Farthest point reached by spacecraft: 12,590 million miles (20,262 million km)—and counting—by Voyager 1

Number of planets: eight

Number of dwarf planets: five

Farthest planet from sun: 2,793 million miles (4,495 million km)

Farthest dwarf planet from sun: 6,289 million miles (10,121 million km)

Largest planet: Jupiter, diameter 88,846 miles (142,984 km)

Smallest planet: Mercury, diameter 3,032 miles (4,880 km)

Distance from our sun to nearest star: 4.2 light-years, Proxima Centauri

S tanding under the sky, it can be hard to grasp that our world speeds through space in a continuous loop, or orbit, around the sun. Meanwhile other objects, some amazingly far away, also orbit that huge, glowing ball. It all holds together because of the sun's strong gravitational pull.

5 COOL FACTS TO RECORD

asteroid belt

Ceres (dwarf planet)

Mars

Venus

Earth

Mercury

Jupiter

sun

A FAMILY OF PLANETS
In this diagram, planets and other objects are to scale but distances between them are not.

1 THE AWESOME SUN
Burning big and bright

The sun is the star of the solar system. In fact, it's almost the entire show! If the solar system were a sumo wrestler holding a couple of handfuls of clay, the sun would be the weight of the wrestler and everything else would be made from the clay.

2 TERRESTRIAL PLANETS
Solid footing

As different as they are, the four planets closest to the sun share something in common: Mercury, Venus, Earth, and Mars are rocky, or terrestrial, planets. Their surfaces are solid.

At Cape Canaveral Air Force Station in Florida, U.S.A., an Atlas V rocket carrying NASA's OSIRIS-REx spacecraft lifts off on September 8, 2016. The spacecraft is on its way to asteroid Bennu to retrieve surface material for study.

TAKE IN THE SUN

From Earth, the sun seems calm, but it is a hotbed of action. This great ball of energy spins like a top, and the outer layer of gas that we see as its "surface" churns and swirls like boiling soup.

JUMP TO JUPITER

On Independence Day, July 4, 2016, planet-watchers and mission teams celebrated as NASA's space probe Juno successfully maneuvered into orbit around Jupiter, after its five-year journey from Earth.

SOAR TO THE SMALLEST

The miniature asteroid called 2012 XB112 is the smallest officially recognized natural space object orbiting the sun. At about 8.2 feet (2.5 m) across, it is about as wide as a small outdoor trampoline.

DIGITAL TRAVELER!

To find a short movie that gives a good sense of the scale of the solar system (if only to Neptune's orbit), search the Internet for "To Scale: The Solar System on Vimeo."

5 LOTS OF OTHER STUFF, TOO

Trillions of specks, chunks, and mountain-size masses of rock, ice, or a mix of both zoom in orbit around the sun. These include asteroids and comets. They are thought to be nearly unchanged from when they first formed billions of years ago.

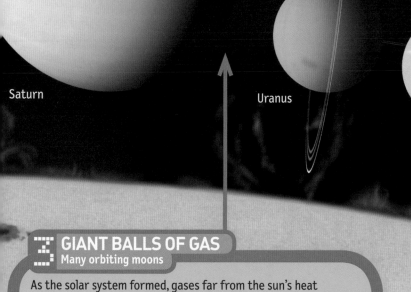

Saturn

Uranus

Neptune

Pluto

Haumea

Makemake

Eris

(four dwarf planets)

3 GIANT BALLS OF GAS
Many orbiting moons

As the solar system formed, gases far from the sun's heat gathered. They formed four gas planets: Jupiter, Saturn, Uranus, and Neptune. Each has many moons orbiting it and rings around it. Like all planets, they don't burn and give out light like a star but instead reflect the sun's light—that's how we can see them.

4 DWARF PLANETS
A class of its own

Pluto is the most famous dwarf planet, but it's not the only one! Ceres, Eris, Haumea, and Makemake join the list of planet-shaped space objects. Dozens more recently discovered objects may soon be added to the list of dwarf planets.

5 COOL FACTS TO RECORD

SPACE TRAVEL INFORMATION

OTHER STAR-PLANET SYSTEMS
Swing by Proxima Centauri, orbited by a planet about the size of Earth. It's the closest planetary system to ours. Also visit Kepler-90, with its seven planets, and planet Kepler-16b, which orbits two stars.

A QUIRKY COINCIDENCE
In the 1700s astronomers noticed that each planet then known was about twice as far from the sun as the one before it. They named this pattern the Titius-Bode Law for the astronomers who found the fact.

VARIETY SHOW
Keep your eyes open from page 40 to 95 for planets with the shortest and longest years (88 days and 247.9 Earth years); the fastest and slowest days (9.9 hours and 243 Earth days); and the hottest and coldest temperatures—864°F (462°C) and −357°F (−216°C).

1 MEASURING DISTANCES
Because of the vast distances between objects in space, it is helpful to use the average distance between Earth and the sun as a standard measure. This distance is known as an astronomical unit, or AU. One AU is equal to 93 million miles (150 million km).

2 INNER SOLAR SYSTEM
Close to the center
Four rocky planets and a band of rocky asteroids are tucked "close" to the sun—if you compare their orbits to those of the outermost planets. The inner solar system is only about one-tenth the size of the outermost planet's orbit. Compared to the entire solar system, which stretches far beyond the planets (see lower part of illustration), the inner solar system is just a tiny sliver.

3 OUTER SOLAR SYSTEM
Far, far away
Stretching more than nine million million miles (14 million million km) from the sun, the outer solar system contains huge gas planets—with numerous moons and swooping rings—along with comets and teeny flecks of dust.

INNER SOLAR SYSTEM

MARS
MERCURY
VENUS
SUN
EARTH

Pluto (dwarf planet)

NEPTUNE

ASTEROID BELT
SUN
Ceres (dwarf planet)
JUPITER
URANUS

SUN CENTERED
Planetary SYSTEMS

Over and over again in our universe, clouds of gas have collapsed to become stars orbited by planets and other objects, such as comets, asteroids, moons, and dwarf planets. We live in an age of incredible discovery about other solar systems in space, but astronomers have managed to describe only our solar system in detail. As we explore space further and gain new information, will we learn that we live in a one-of-a-kind system—or that ours is not so different after all? It will be exciting to find out.

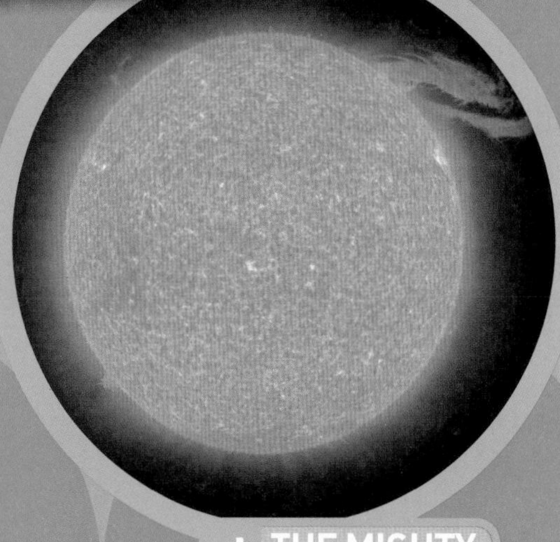

4 THE MIGHTY SUN

Our sun rules supreme. It has almost all of the matter in the solar system, and its pull of gravity keeps even the farthest solar system objects orbiting it. In addition, its energy affects weather, magnetism, and electricity on Earth, and its warmth is powerful enough to melt ice in the outer reaches of the solar system. Its other forms of radiation help us understand the nature of stars and the wonders of space (see pages 8 and 36–39).

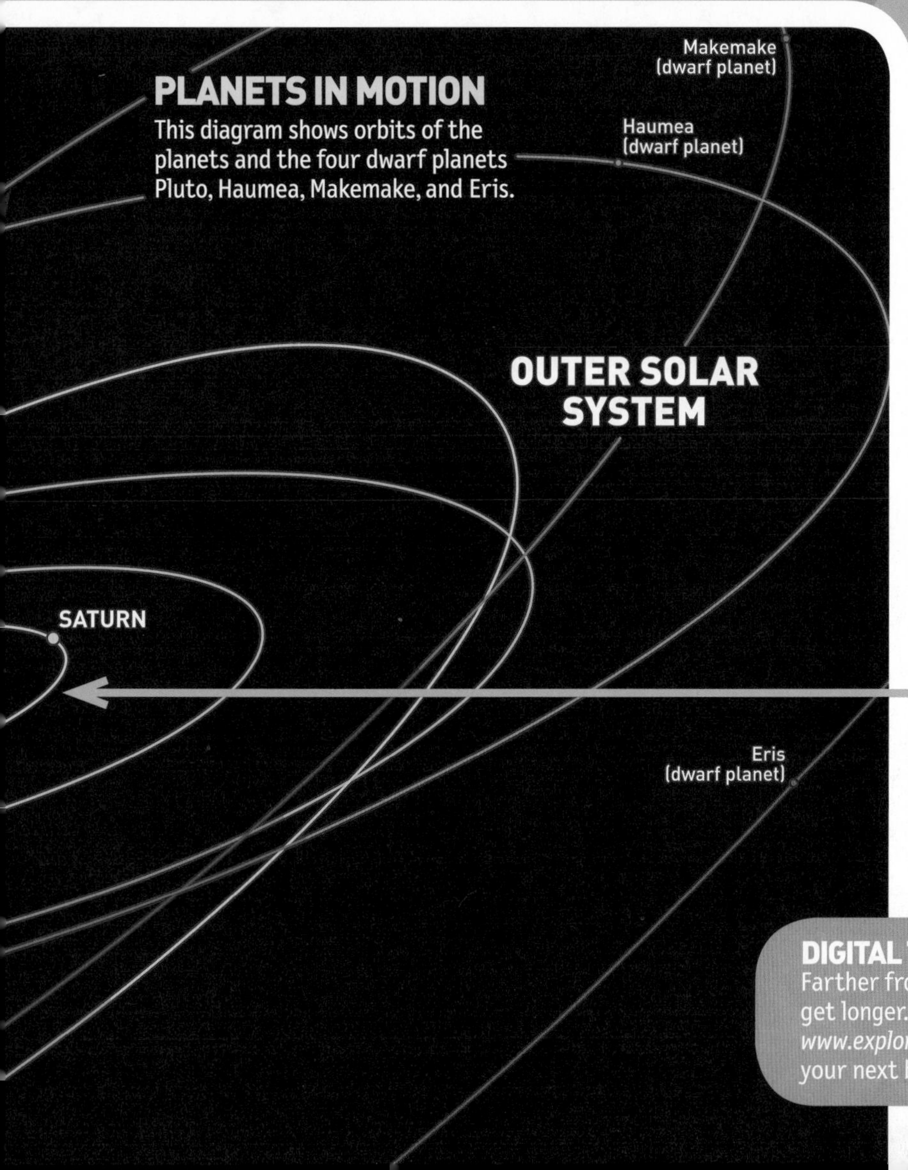

PLANETS IN MOTION

This diagram shows orbits of the planets and the four dwarf planets Pluto, Haumea, Makemake, and Eris.

Makemake
(dwarf planet)

Haumea
(dwarf planet)

OUTER SOLAR SYSTEM

SATURN

Eris
(dwarf planet)

5 LOOPS AROUND THE SUN
Orbital paths

The planets and other space objects orbit counterclockwise in this diagram. Most planets' orbits are almost exactly on the same level as each other, although some objects, such as the dwarf planets and several comets, can have sharply sloped orbits.

DIGITAL TRAVELER!

Farther from the sun, orbits are bigger and years get longer. To get a sense of this go to the website *www.exploratorium.edu/ronh/age* and find out your next birthday on other planets.

INNER SOLAR SYSTEM

Swinging close to the SUN

Our planet and our moon, along with the sun, three other planets and their moons, and many asteroids are located in the inner solar system. Here, rocks rule. You'll find lots of solid ground. In fact, Mercury, Venus, Earth, and Mars are called terrestrial planets based on the Latin, *terra*, which means earth, or ground. Compared to the outer planets, the inner planets are smaller and huddle close to the sun as they orbit it. Location, size, and structure unite these inner solar system bodies, but the more you get to know them the more you will see that each is unique. Welcome to your local space neighborhood.

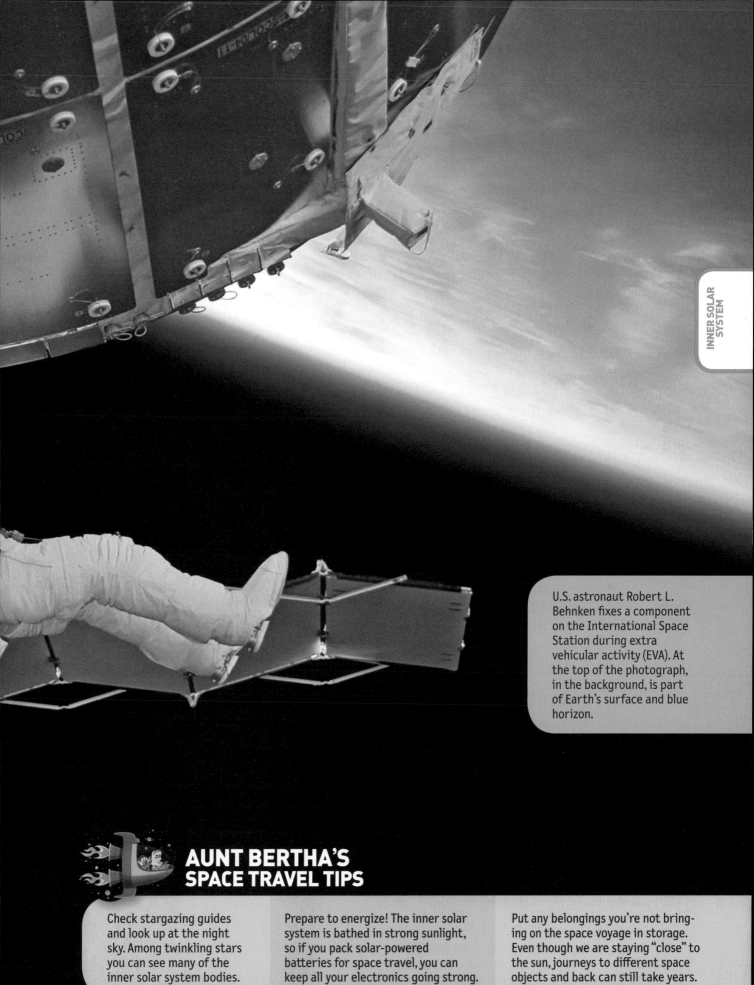

U.S. astronaut Robert L. Behnken fixes a component on the International Space Station during extra vehicular activity (EVA). At the top of the photograph, in the background, is part of Earth's surface and blue horizon.

AUNT BERTHA'S
SPACE TRAVEL TIPS

Check stargazing guides and look up at the night sky. Among twinkling stars you can see many of the inner solar system bodies.

Prepare to energize! The inner solar system is bathed in strong sunlight, so if you pack solar-powered batteries for space travel, you can keep all your electronics going strong.

Put any belongings you're not bringing on the space voyage in storage. Even though we are staying "close" to the sun, journeys to different space objects and back can still take years.

MIGHTY SUN

Burning BRIGHT

Like any star, our sun is basically a giant, spinning ball of gases. The outer material, thousands of miles (km) thick, presses in on the sun's center. There, atoms—the tiny building blocks of all matter—are packed as close as atoms can get ... and then some. This pressure causes atoms to merge, or fuse—something that cannot happen under most conditions. This fusion converts just a minute bit of matter into an enormous amount of energy. This is the energy we see, feel, detect (with special sensors), and recognize as our sun.

1 WAY TO GLOW

Just how bright is sunshine? Every second, the sun emits visible light that is brighter than 1,500,000,000,000,000, 000,000,000 (that's 1.5 trillion trillion) 100-watt lightbulbs. It takes eight minutes for this light to reach Earth.

TIME TRAVELER!

In the future, Earthlings might rely on the superpowered sun as a major source of energy. A space-based system of shiny balloon reflectors and laser beams might direct solar energy to the ground.

SPACE TRAVEL ATTRACTIONS

2 RADIANT ENERGY

The sun bathes space with all the different forms of light—which have electrical and magnetic properties—including low-energy radio waves, warming infrared "heat," visible light, X-rays, and the most energetic, dangerous gamma rays. They alter the chemicals found on the planets and in living things on Earth.

CHILL OUT CLOSE TO THE SURFACE

Imagine approaching a bonfire. You feel hot, hotter, then scorching as you move closer. Weirdly, that's not the case in the sun's inner atmosphere. Far out, the temperature is millions of degrees. As you get closer to the surface, the temperature drops to around 10,000°F (about 5500°C).

WATCH FOR WEATHER ALERTS

Hang out at the orbiting space-based Solar and Heliospheric Observatory (SOHO). It's built for science, but it's also a space meteorology machine. It sends space weather alerts when solar activity threatens Earth's sensitive satellites, power grids, and communications networks.

GO COMET-WATCHING

The sun's strong gravity reels in comets from the far reaches of the solar system. With SOHO and other instruments, scientists have discovered thousands of comets zooming near the sun.

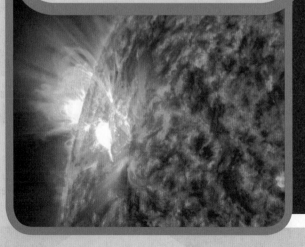

3 THERE IT GLOWS AGAIN
The photosphere

We see only the top 1/7,000 of the sun. This 62-mile (100-km)-deep area is called the photosphere. The photosphere is where energy released at the core of the sun heats up gases to high temperatures so they glow like a candle flame.

4 SPACE WEATHER

As gigantic solar explosions spew intense energy and matter in massive bursts, they create space weather. A feature of this weather is a shifting solar wind of electrically charged particles. The wind relentlessly streams out from the sun in all directions at one million miles an hour (1.6 million km/h). It causes interference in radio transmissions and power outages on Earth.

INNER SOLAR SYSTEM

SUN DATA

Orbital period: not applicable
Rotational period: 26.8 Earth days at the Equator, 36 Earth days at the Poles
Diameter: 864,337 miles (1,391,016 km)
Mass: 330,060 Earth's
Density (water=1): 1.4
Gravity at surface: 0.28 Earth's
Surface temperature: 9939°F (5504°C)
Satellites: eight planets and their moons, five dwarf planets, more than one million asteroids

Earth   sun

5 GETTING LOOPY
Solar prominences

Responding to powerful magnetic forces, glowing plasma (electrically charged gas) spouts from the sun's surface, forming loops called prominences. The largest ones extend hundreds of thousands of miles (km) into space before arcing back to the sun's surface.

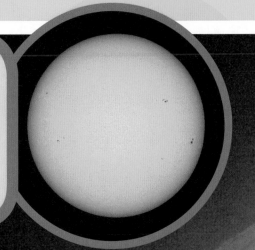

A CHURNING BALL of GAS

A riot of raging energy, winds, and STORMS

Ulysses flies past the sun

From Earth, the sun may look simply like a glowing ball. But this multilayered mammoth—the size of 1.3 million Earths—is an ever changing frenzy of heat, light, and motion fueled by its core.

As atoms fuse there, the resulting energy echoes outward. Searing-hot gases churn. Magnetic storms rage. The solar wind flows, and outbursts of X-rays and clouds of charged matter surge. From a safe distance of 93 million miles (about 150 million km) away, we take in the sunshine while our atmosphere absorbs the most dangerous radiation. With light traveling at 186,000 miles a second (299,338 km/s), the sun's radiation takes eight minutes to reach Earth.

COOL FACTS TO RECORD

INVISIBLE VEIL OF GAS

The sun's thinly spread atmosphere, the corona, surrounds it as a halo. Usually invisible, it shows itself during a solar eclipse, when the moon blocks the ultrabright light of the photosphere. Can't wait for an eclipse? Use a specialized telescope, a coronagraph, to block out the sun and reveal the halo.

WATCH THE STEW BREW

Watching the sun's convective zone close-up, you might think of simmering soup. The searing core acts like a stove burner, heating a plasma stew (charged gases). Like bubbling soup, the hot plasma rises from the base of the zone toward the solar surface, where it cools, gets denser, sinks back to the bottom, and gets heated again. Then this convection process starts again.

CORE OF DARKNESS

Take a dive from the blindingly bright photosphere deep into the sun's core, and get ready for what you would see: nothing. All the light energy there is in the form of invisible X-rays. The core would look pitch black.

SUNSPOTS
The photosphere

Giant magnetic storms on the sun's surface create an ever changing pattern of dark sunspots. Earth could easily fit inside a single average sunspot. Because the spots are cooler than their surroundings—only 6200°F (3427°C) compared to 9800°F (5427°C)—they don't glow as brightly.

SOLAR EXPLOSION
Solar flares

In a gigantic burst, a solar flare releases tremendous amounts of high-energy rays, which pour outward at the speed of light. These solar flares can affect signals on Earth. Eight minutes later, you might hear the result as a poor cell phone signal.

DIGITAL TRAVELER!

It's never safe to look directly at the sun—unless you are viewing it online. Check out what the sun is up to with daily videos and snapshots. *sohowww.nascom.nasa.gov/data/realtime/mpeg*

TIGHT SQUEEZE
Nuclear core

The core takes up less than 2 percent of all the space in the sun—but 50 percent of the sun's matter is crammed into it. This jam-packed, dense environment forces the nuclei of hydrogen atoms to fuse, making helium.

WHERE X-RAYS PLAY PINBALL
Radiative zone

X-rays move from the core of the sun through the dense radiative zone. If this layer were empty, these rays could cross in a second. However, they keep bumping into particles, taking a zigzagging, one-million-year journey out to the surface of the sun.

MAGNETIC GENERATOR
Tachocline

The sun's magnetic field is one of its major features. The magnetic field is thought to begin in the tachocline. This thin, middle layer of the sun is rich with charged particles and gases. When electric charges move, they generate magnetism.

an illustration showing the inner structure and outer surface of the sun

COOL FACTS TO RECORD

SPACE TRAVEL ATTRACTIONS

1 NO ATMOSPHERE

Mercury has no true atmosphere, only the thinnest smattering of a few gas molecules near ground level. The molecules boil off from the surface and ultimately drift into space.

↪ SOLAR WIND EFFECTS

Mercury has a magnetic field, but a navigational compass would probably go haywire there, thanks to the interfering solar wind. It's 10 times stronger at Mercury than at Earth.

↪ BIRTHDAY BOOTY

Mercury's orbit takes about three months—one-quarter of an Earth year. That means you could celebrate your birthday four times more often if you lived on Mercury.

↪ MOONLESS SKYSCAPE, SUPERSIZED SUN

Mercury is one of only two planets in the solar system without a moon to call its own. (Venus is the other.) However, by day, the sun is a fantastic sight, about triple the size we see from Earth.

2 ALL ROCK, ALL THE TIME

Although it's all rock, Mercury displays a range of landscape features, including craters, mountains, plains, valleys, and a type of cliff called *rupes*.

MERCURY DATA

Orbital period: 88 Earth days
Rotational period: 58.7 Earth days
Diameter: 3,032 miles (4,880 km)
Mass: 0.06 Earth's
Density (water=1): 5.4
Gravity: 0.38 Earth's
Average distance from sun:
    36 million miles (57.9 million km)
Surface temperature: −279°F
    (−173°C) to 801°F (427°C)
Moons: none

Earth   Mercury

an artist's impression of the sun as viewed from the vast craters of the planet Mercury

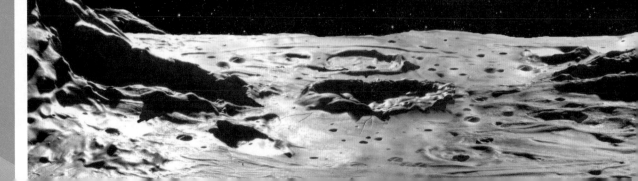

MINI MERCURY

A world of EXTREMES

DID YOU KNOW?

Because Mercury's orbital path is not what early astronomers predicted, some looked for another planet closer to the sun that could be Mercury—and thought they found it. But the "planet" was just a sunspot.

Mercury lies close to the sun and so is bathed in solar glare. As a result, this innermost planet is mostly hidden from Earth's view. Mercury is a scorching planet, yet it is thought to hold ice. Its magnetic field is very weak, and its orbit is strangely oval in shape. Mercury is rocky and cratered, and lacks a true atmosphere. It also has several unique features: It's the *smallest* planet; it's *closest* to the sun; and it has the *wildest* temperature swings. Its surface is the *oldest,* and its inner core is the *largest* of its kind.

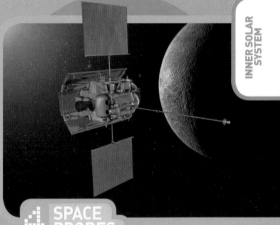

INNER SOLAR SYSTEM

4 SPACE PROBES

Two probes have flown by Mercury. Mariner 10 provided the first close-up views in 1974. Almost 40 years later, MESSENGER—as in this impression—followed and mapped it for four years.

DIGITAL TRAVELER!

Want to soar over the surface of Mercury, or watch as it spins against a black backdrop? Go to the website *messenger.jhuapl.edu* and click on "Explore" to see MESSENGER probe videos.

5 REMAINS OF THE DEAD

Ghost craters are traces of ancient planetary history. Lava flooded and buried these old meteorite-impact craters, whose rims are just barely visible.

3 EXPLOSIVE ERUPTIONS

Recently, scientists were surprised to find signs that forceful volcanoes once erupted on Mercury. Bright orange areas on this MESSENGER image mark the position of vents where hot lava shot out from the surface in enormous, glowing sprays.

A WEIRD WORLD

A small planet full of SURPRISES

Imagine aliens studying Earth but only from a distance and visiting just twice. What would they see—and miss? That's our situation with Mercury. Mariner 10, the first Mercury probe, completed three flybys of the planet. It captured fascinating glimpses of the surface and clued us in to Mercury's weak magnetic field. But it didn't prepare us for the surprises. MESSENGER revealed signs of a liquid core, explosive volcanic eruptions, and big, recent changes on a small planet that should have stopped changing long ago.

MESSENGER

5 COOL FACTS TO RECORD

1 CRATERS AND BASINS
Caloris Basin

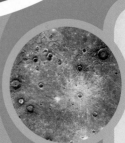

Stretching about as wide as the Gulf of Mexico, Caloris Basin is one of Mercury's many asteroid impact sites, and one of the solar system's largest. Areas at its edge show evidence of past explosive volcanic eruptions.

one face of **MERCURY**

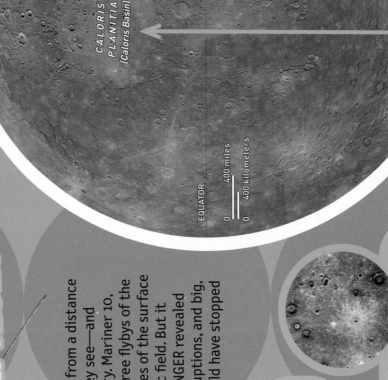

North Pole

BOREALIS
PLANITIA

SUISEI
PLANITIA

SOBKOU
PLANITIA

ODIN
PLANITIA

BUDH
PLANITIA

CALORIS
PLANITIA
(Caloris Basin)

TIR PLANITIA

Hero Rupes

Beethoven

South Pole

EQUATOR

0   400 miles

0   400 kilometers

North Pole

*BOREALIS
PLANITIA*

Hokusai ◇

*CALORIS
ANTIPODAL
TERRAIN
(Weird Terrain)*

Debussy ◇

South Pole

EQUATOR

0   400 miles
0   400 kilometers

On planet maps, features are often given Latin names. *Planitia* is a flat area, like a basin within an impact site, and *rupes* is a cliff. On some planets, craters are named after famous people, such as the musician Beethoven.

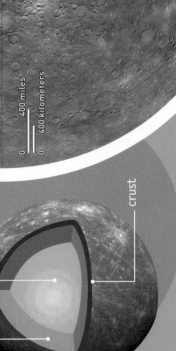

core

mantle

crust

⁵ MESSENGER PROBE

This probe's name stands for MErcury Surface, Space ENvironment, GEochemistry, and Ranging. The spacecraft scanned almost the entire surface of the planet. In four Earth years, it orbited 4,014 times and took more than 277,000 images.

INNER SOLAR
SYSTEM

² ONE-OF-A-KIND LOCATION
Weird terrain

Swing to the other side of the planet from Caloris Basin and you'll find what scientists nicknamed the "Weird Terrain." Scientists think this irregular, hilly area was caused by an intense shock wave following the same impact that carved out the grand Caloris Basin.

³ INNER STRUCTURE

Mercury's core is huge—about three-quarters the size of its diameter. That's like the amount of juicy flesh in a grapefruit compared to its peel. (Earth's core is about half its own diameter.) Scientists speculate that early in its history, Mercury's outer layers were blown away during an impact or burned away by the sun.

⁴ BEPICOLOMBO MISSION

Due to arrive in 2024, BepiColombo is the next planned mission to Mercury. It will include two orbiters equipped with 18 instruments in total. It is a joint mission between European and Japanese space agencies.

surface of Venus

RED, HOT VENUS

An atmosphere of ACID

Before scientists investigated Venus close-up, people imagined a tropical planet. In reality, its thick cloak of clouds hides a harsh world. Thunder roars, lightning flashes, and tornado-speed winds rip through clouds of sulfuric acid. At ground level, it's hot enough to melt lead. Venus's atmosphere is so thick that a slow-moving wind is like a strong, invisible wave, powerful enough to topple you—if its pressure doesn't crush you first. Sulfuric acid raindrops fall from the sky and vaporize before reaching the surface. Venus is one hot, dense, fascinating planet.

SPACE TRAVEL ATTRACTIONS

▶ RARE SUNRISE
On Venus, the sun rises and sets just once every 177 Earth days. Venus spins backward compared to Earth, so the sun rises in the west and sets in the east.

▶ UNRELENTING HEAT
Even though Venus is not closest to the sun, the planet's 40-mile (64.4-km)-thick cloud layer insulates the planet, sealing in extreme heat. Surface conditions are a steady 864°F (462°C), day and night, giving Venus the solar system record for highest surface temperature.

▶ TIGHT SQUEEZE
Does Venus—named for the Roman goddess of love—have a crush on you? It would if you visited. With an atmospheric pressure 90 times as great as Earth's, Venus would squish you.

1 TRANSITS OF VENUS

On June 6, 2012, a rare but regular transit of Venus took place. A transit occurs when a planet crosses between Earth and the sun and appears as a dark spot creeping across the sun's face. You might get a chance to see the next transit of Venus on December 11, 2117—but remember to view the sun through solar filters.

2 SHINING BRIGHT

On Earth, Venus has often been reported as a UFO, possibly because it appears so bright. Only the sun and moon outshine it. It can be spotted near sunrise or sunset, although sharp-eyed observers can see Venus even in daytime's bright light.

3 WILD WEATHER IN THE CLOUDS

Far above the surface of Venus, winds race around at 50 times the speed of the planet's spin on its axis. Windblown clouds interact with the solar wind, creating magnetic effects. Spacecraft have detected lightning on Venus, as in this artist's impression.

5 COOL FACTS TO RECORD

4 VOLCANIC SURFACE

Shield volcanoes, cone volcanoes, big volcanoes, small volcanoes. They're all here. Recent evidence from mineral, atmosphere, and temperature studies (like this colorized temperature scan) suggests that there's volcanic activity on Venus.

5 BAD BREATH

Suppose for a moment you could avoid being crushed by Venus's thick atmosphere and burned by its acidic rain. What then? Breathing its air, which is mostly carbon dioxide, would suffocate you.

An artist's impression shows sunlight reflected from Venus's clouds, making its crescent shine brightly.

VENUS DATA

Orbital period: 224.7 Earth days
Rotational period: 243 Earth days
Diameter: 7,521 miles (12,104 km)
Mass: 0.82 Earth's
Density (water=1): 5.2
Gravity: 0.91 Earth's
Average distance from sun:
    67.2 million miles (108.2 million km)
Surface temperature: 864°F (462°C)
Moons: none

Earth

Venus

DIGITAL TRAVELER!

To keep tabs on ideas for a possible future mission to Venus, search the Internet for NASA's Venus Flagship, which might include one orbiter, two landers, and two cloud-bound balloons.
vfm.jpl.nasa.gov

INNER SOLAR SYSTEM

45

A VOLCANIC WORLD

A greenhouse ATMOSPHERE

2 THE INSIDE STORY

If you shrank Venus to the size of a Ping-Pong ball, its core would be marble-size. The rest of the ball would be the mantle, and the crust would be about as thick as one or two coats of paint on the surface.

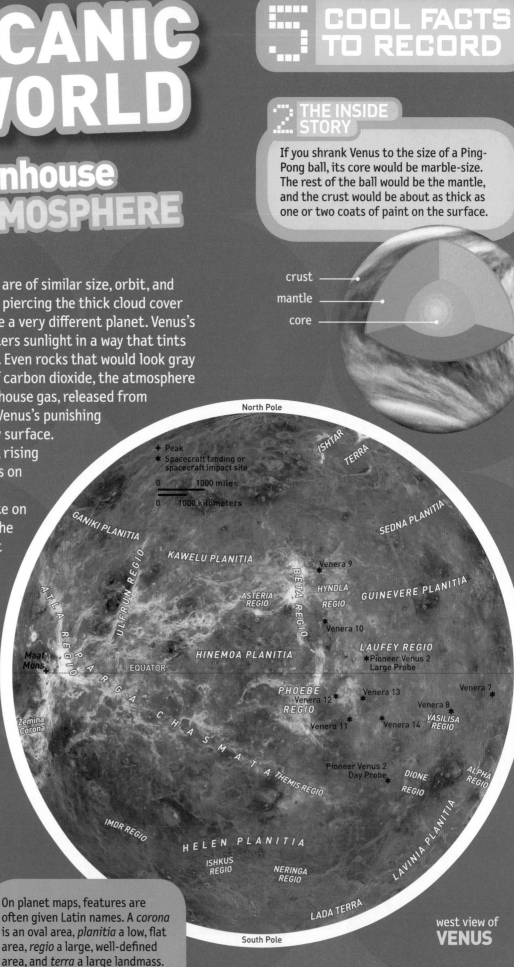

crust
mantle
core

Venus and Earth are of similar size, orbit, and mass. But after piercing the thick cloud cover of Venus, we see a very different planet. Venus's atmosphere filters sunlight in a way that tints everything red. Even rocks that would look gray on Earth look ruddy. Full of carbon dioxide, the atmosphere also traps heat. This greenhouse gas, released from volcanoes, contributes to Venus's punishing temperature and bone-dry surface. It's thought that, long ago, rising temperatures dried oceans on Venus similar to the way backyard puddles evaporate on Earth at high noon, when the sun's heat is intense. It left behind a waterless, volcanic landscape.

1 DOOMED LANDERS

Many spacecraft that have attempted to land on Venus have crashed, been crushed, or burned. When the Soviet Venera 7 survived, it became the first craft to send data from the surface. Even successful missions have been doomed, lasting only a few short hours in Venus's high-pressure atmosphere and intense heat.

On planet maps, features are often given Latin names. A *corona* is an oval area, *planitia* a low, flat area, *regio* a large, well-defined area, and *terra* a large landmass.

North Pole

+ Peak
* Spacecraft landing or spacecraft impact site

0   1000 miles
0   1000 kilometers

GANIKI PLANITIA

ULFRUN REGIO

KAWELU PLANITIA

ATLA REGIO

ASTERIA REGIO

BETA REGIO

HYNDLA REGIO

GUINEVERE PLANITIA

ISHTAR TERRA

SEDNA PLANITIA

Venera 9

Venera 10

LAUFEY REGIO

Maat Mons

PARGA CHASMATA

HINEMOA PLANITIA

EQUATOR

Pioneer Venus 2 Large Probe

Žemina Corona

PHOEBE REGIO

Venera 12

Venera 13

Venera 8

Venera 7

VASILISA REGIO

Venera 11

Venera 14

THEMIS REGIO

Pioneer Venus 2 Day Probe

DIONE REGIO

ALPHA REGIO

IMDR REGIO

HELEN PLANITIA

ISHKUS REGIO

NERINGA REGIO

LAVINIA PLANITIA

LADA TERRA

South Pole

west view of **VENUS**

3 CRATER CHRONICLES

Venus lacks small craters because small meteorites that would create them burn up in Venus's extra-thick atmosphere. It also has fewer large craters than expected, probably because newer lava has replaced an older surface.

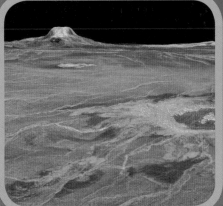

DIGITAL TRAVELER!

Sure, sending a spacecraft to Venus is a big deal, but for a real challenge, try making a paper model of the European Space Agency's Venus Express probe. Go to the web page *esamultimedia.esa.int/images/ venusexpress/Venus_Express_Model_ Instruction.pdf* to download the manual.

DID YOU KNOW?

Venus has helped scientists explore Mercury. On Mariner 10's two flybys of Venus, the planet's gravitational pull on the spacecraft slowed it down. This helped Mariner 10 enter Mercury's orbit. This spaceflight technique is known as a gravity assist maneuver.

4 BLOBS FROM BELOW

Round, flat-shaped areas called domes probably formed when extra-thick lava rose from under the level ground, spread like gooey batter into an even layer, and then cooled.

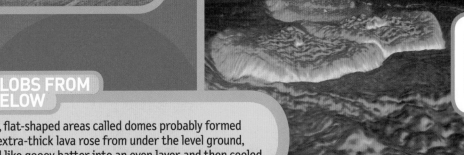

INNER SOLAR SYSTEM

5 MAGELLAN ORBITER

Safe from Venus's harsh conditions, orbiters such as NASA's Magellan—seen here in a space shuttle bay—fare better than landers. Between 1990 and 1994, Magellan's cloud-piercing radar and high-resolution imaging allowed it to map more than 98 percent of Venus's surface, revealing volcanoes and impact craters.

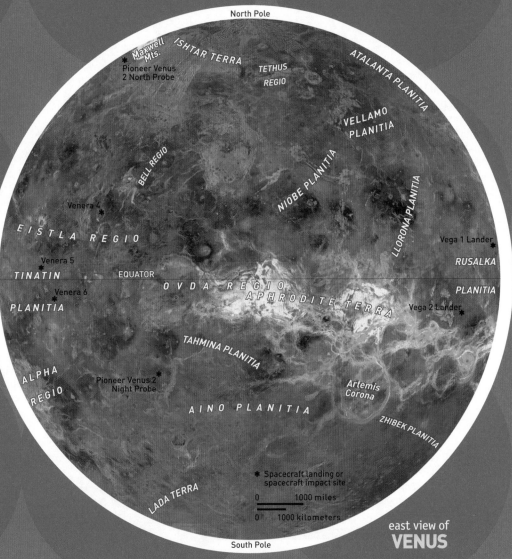

North Pole

Maxwell Mts.
Pioneer Venus 2 North Probe
ISHTAR TERRA
TETHUS REGIO
ATALANTA PLANITIA
VELLAMO PLANITIA
BELL REGIO
NIOBE PLANITIA
LLORONA PLANITIA
Venera 4
EISTLA REGIO
Vega 1 Lander
RUSALKA
Venera 5
TINATIN
EQUATOR
OVDA REGIO
PLANITIA
Venera 6
APHRODITE TERRA
PLANITIA
Vega 2 Lander
TAHMINA PLANITIA
ALPHA REGIO
Pioneer Venus 2 Night Probe
Artemis Corona
AINO PLANITIA
ZHIBEK PLANITIA

★ Spacecraft landing or spacecraft impact site

0   1000 miles
0   1000 kilometers

LADA TERRA

south Pole

east view of
VENUS

47

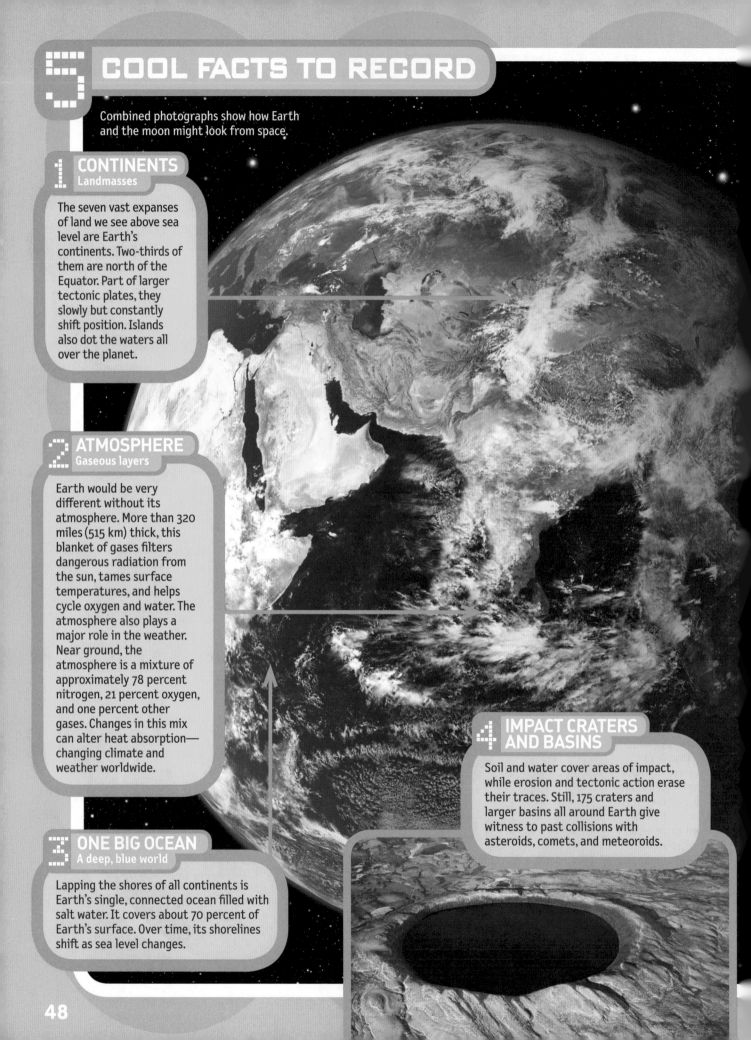

Combined photographs show how Earth and the moon might look from space.

1 CONTINENTS
Landmasses

The seven vast expanses of land we see above sea level are Earth's continents. Two-thirds of them are north of the Equator. Part of larger tectonic plates, they slowly but constantly shift position. Islands also dot the waters all over the planet.

2 ATMOSPHERE
Gaseous layers

Earth would be very different without its atmosphere. More than 320 miles (515 km) thick, this blanket of gases filters dangerous radiation from the sun, tames surface temperatures, and helps cycle oxygen and water. The atmosphere also plays a major role in the weather. Near ground, the atmosphere is a mixture of approximately 78 percent nitrogen, 21 percent oxygen, and one percent other gases. Changes in this mix can alter heat absorption—changing climate and weather worldwide.

4 IMPACT CRATERS AND BASINS

Soil and water cover areas of impact, while erosion and tectonic action erase their traces. Still, 175 craters and larger basins all around Earth give witness to past collisions with asteroids, comets, and meteoroids.

3 ONE BIG OCEAN
A deep, blue world

Lapping the shores of all continents is Earth's single, connected ocean filled with salt water. It covers about 70 percent of Earth's surface. Over time, its shorelines shift as sea level changes.

PLANET EARTH

Third rock from the SUN

New York

INNER SOLAR SYSTEM

5 GLOWING SKIES

The planet's magnetic field directs solar wind particles, contributing to one of the best shows on Earth—the vibrant northern lights and southern lights (aurora borealis and aurora australis).

Covered with water and brimming with life, Earth hardly seems like the other rocky planets. But there are some similarities. There are high plateaus sloping to ocean beds, volcanoes, and impact basins. Earth also spins on an axis, has a moon, and orbits the sun. What makes the planet so unique is the water and atmosphere that allow life to thrive.

EARTH DATA

Orbital period: 365.24 Earth days
Rotational period: 23.9 hours
Diameter: 7,926 miles (12,756 km)
Mass: 6,580 billion billion tons (5,969 billion billion t)
Density (water=1): 5.5
Average distance from sun: 93 million miles (149.6 million km)
Surface temperature: −126°F (−88°C) to 136°F (58°C)
Moons: one

Earth   moon

SPACE TRAVEL ATTRACTIONS

GET YOUR FEET WET
Splash in the ocean, ski a glacier, sing in the rain, and drink up. Earth's plentiful water makes it a one-of-a-kind planet.

ENJOY LIFE!
Earth is the only place in the universe where we know life exists. Our world is host to about two million identified species (with an estimated 10 to 20 million more waiting for discovery).

A WORLD IN ACTION
Tour the planet with a geologist's eye. Earth's active tectonic plates are rocky, often continent-size slabs of rock. Their interactions create volcanoes, raise mountains, and cause earthquakes.

WATER, AIR, AND LAND

The planet that supports LIFE

L ife is everywhere on Earth. It's in dark ocean depths—where searing lava pours from cracks in the planet's crust—in deserts, and in frigid ice caps. It's on mountain peaks, deep within rocks, and even in the clouds! All life on Earth depends on the chemicals in its rocks, water, and atmosphere for survival. Earth's tilt and rotation contribute to blowing winds and flowing ocean currents that transport seeds, microbes, and nutrients worldwide. Meanwhile, the motion of Earth's crust changes the environment. Earth impacts life, and life changes and shapes Earth.

1 POLAR CAPS
Cold storage

White ice caps averaging about one mile (1.6 km) deep at Earth's poles currently hold about 70 percent of the planet's freshwater. Despite the cold, life exists here—microbes survive by eating rock.

5 COOL FACTS TO RECORD

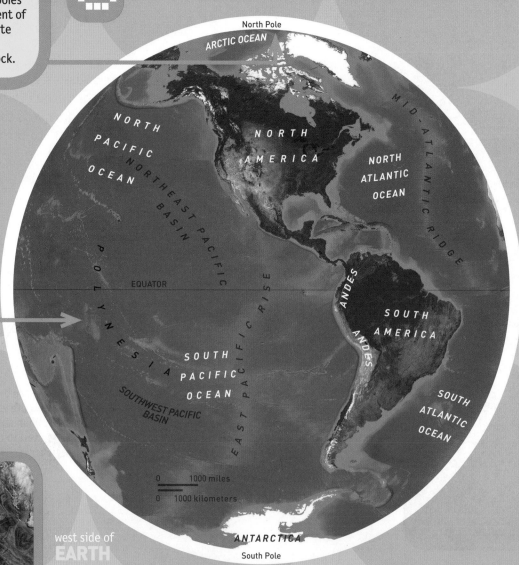

North Pole

ARCTIC OCEAN

NORTH PACIFIC OCEAN

NORTHEAST PACIFIC BASIN

NORTH AMERICA

MID-ATLANTIC RIDGE

NORTH ATLANTIC OCEAN

EQUATOR

POLYNESIA

EAST PACIFIC RISE

ANDES

SOUTH AMERICA

SOUTH PACIFIC OCEAN

SOUTHWEST PACIFIC BASIN

SOUTH ATLANTIC OCEAN

0   1000 miles

0   1000 kilometers

ANTARCTICA

South Pole

west side of EARTH

2 OCEAN CURRENTS
Follow the flow

On the ocean surface and deep below, currents are riverlike flows of water. Driven by wind, the Earth's rotation, and differences in ocean temperature, the currents constantly change the distribution of nutrients and life-forms in the oceans.

4 INSIDE STORY

Earth is the only planet currently known to have a crust broken into tectonic plates. The plates slide over the mantle. In the outer core, motion of liquified nickel and iron creates the Earth's magnetic field. An inner core is made mostly of solid iron.

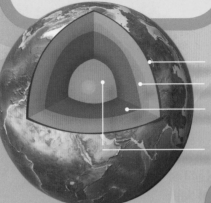

crust
mantle
outer core
inner core

DID YOU KNOW?

Scientists are now investigating a "shadow biosphere" on Earth, a system of life-forms that depend on nonstandard chemical processes. Some viruses survive in this way—they do not depend on water, oxygen, and proteins. Learning about such organisms could help us think about possible life on other planets.

INNER SOLAR SYSTEM

3 FORESTS
Green blankets

Earth is the only planet in our solar system with forests. These big, sweeping, tree-filled areas burst with life. Tropical rain forests are thought to support about half of Earth's millions of species.

DIGITAL TRAVELER!
No planet is as well mapped as Earth. Watch Earth's land, air, water, and life change over time with the animated maps at *earthobservatory.nasa.gov/GlobalMaps*.

5 DESERTS
Bone dry land

From icy Antarctica to the sandy Sahara, deserts cover about one-third of Earth's land area. Although parched, with minimal rain, all but Antarctica are known to support a wide variety of life. Many deserts contain fossils of dinosaurs, which went extinct more than 65 million years ago.

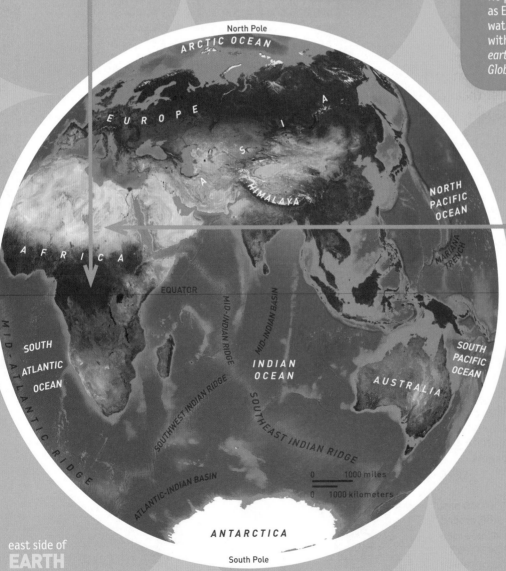

North Pole
ARCTIC OCEAN
EUROPE
ASIA
HIMALAYA
AFRICA
NORTH PACIFIC OCEAN
MARIANA TRENCH
EQUATOR
MID-INDIAN BASIN
SOUTH ATLANTIC OCEAN
MID-ATLANTIC RIDGE
MID-INDIAN RIDGE
INDIAN OCEAN
SOUTHWEST INDIAN RIDGE
SOUTHEAST INDIAN RIDGE
AUSTRALIA
SOUTH PACIFIC OCEAN
ATLANTIC-INDIAN BASIN

0   1000 miles
0   1000 kilometers

ANTARCTICA
South Pole

east side of
EARTH

ORBITING EARTH

Floating on the edge of SPACE

Spend time looking up on a clear night and you might catch one of a fleet of human-made satellites circling Earth—a point of light steadily moving across the sky, then winking out of sight. Some of these orbiters relay cell phone messages and navigation signals. Others help us explore space or our own planet. The International Space Station (ISS) is an orbiter that acts as a home for astronauts living in space.

SPACE TRAVEL ATTRACTIONS

HANG OUT ON AN ORBITER
On the ISS, have fun with microgravity's effects as you gulp floating spheres of orange juice, somersault where there's no upside down, or experiment with static electric effects that make floating water droplets dance in loops around objects.

SPACE WALK
Gear up and drop outside an orbiting space station. Then float completely free in space as a one-person satellite orbiting Earth. Enjoy the ever changing views.

SPACE JUNK
Be careful to avoid the 500,000 or so human-made objects in orbit around Earth. Space junk items include used rocket parts, broken or damaged space equipment, and tiny flecks of paint.

5 COOL FACTS TO RECORD

1 SPACE STATIONS
Way, way over the rainbow

The International Space Station is the biggest and longest-running space station, housing astronauts since 2000. Able to support six crew members at once, ISS has hosted more than 200 astronauts from 15 different nations.

TIME TRAVELER!
In the future, robotic "spiders" may build astronomy equipment in space. Scientists envision these spiders unpacking supplies and assembling them like toy construction sets—some as long as several city blocks—while floating freely in Earth's orbit.

2 BLAST OFF!

As gases stream from their tail ends, rockets zoom forward. Launching astronauts to ISS, rockets reach 18,000 miles an hour (28,968 km/h) in about 10 minutes. Right now, many parts of rockets are single-use items, discarded after launch.

3 SPUTNIK 1 SATELLITE

In 1957, the first human-made satellite, Sputnik 1, was launched into space. On Earth, people tuned in to radios and heard its beeping transmissions. Sputnik 1 orbited Earth every 98 minutes for three months before burning up on reentry into Earth's atmosphere.

International Space Station floating above Earth

4 SPACE SHUTTLES

The 1981 to 2011 U.S. space shuttle program featured reusable vehicles that ferried astronauts and cargo to and from space, orbited, and landed back on Earth like an airplane. Four of these orbiters are displayed at museums in the United States.

5 MISSION TO EARTH

More than 100 artificial satellites orbit Earth. They provide a 24/7 stream of data about plant growth, weather, ocean temperatures, lava flows, and the movement of all kinds of vehicles. This Aura satellite orbits 438 miles (705 km) above Earth about 14 times a day.

MOON DATA

Orbital period: around Earth, 27.3 Earth days; around sun, 365.24
Rotational period: 27.3 Earth days
Diameter: 2,159 miles (3,475 km)
Mass: 0.01 Earth's
Density (water=1): 3.3
Gravity: 0.17 Earth's
Average distance from Earth: 239,000 miles (384,633 km)
Surface temperature: −387°F (−233°C) to 253°F (123°C)

Earth   moon

DIGITAL TRAVELER!
Go on a moon mission. Search the Internet for NASA's Apollo moon landing videos at *nasa.gov/ multimedia/hd/apollo11_hdpage.html.*

5 ANCIENT CREATION

It is thought that the moon was created as a result of a Mars-size space object crashing into Earth about 4.5 billion years ago—as in this artist's impression. At the time, Earth was molten rock, or magma. Some of the splattered magma thrown up formed a blob that gradually cooled and hardened.

moon landing and surface equipment, July 20, 1969

4 POWDERY SURFACE

A layer of powdery moon rock covers the lunar surface, hinting at past collisions with tiny meteorites. The footprints of moon pioneers, Neil Armstrong and Edwin "Buzz" Aldrin, provide a sense of the rock's texture.

3 THIN AIR

The moon's atmosphere differs greatly from Earth's. It is far less dense. Also, it has an unusual mix of gases, such as sodium and potassium, which are detected as a glow by a special telescope placed on the moon.

THE MOON

lunar rover

Earth's constant COMPANION

DID YOU KNOW?

Not only is there water on the moon, but NASA researchers are also investigating a unique, lunar-style water cycle. Water is present on the entire surface for at least part of the lunar day.

5 COOL FACTS TO RECORD

Barring obstacles and bad weather on Earth, you can see our moon from anywhere on the planet, almost every day of the year. It takes the moon the same amount of time to spin on its axis as it does to orbit around Earth—27.3 Earth days. As a result, we see only one of its faces. With just our eyes, we can see bright and dark patches in patterns. Some of us see a man in the moon, others a toad or rabbit. The bright patches are highlands, the dark ones are the moon's "seas"—impact craters filled with lava (see page 56). Closer inspection through an average telescope reveals stark details of spike-edged craters, flat basins of frozen lava, and mountain peaks.

1 LUNAR TERMINATOR

As the moon regularly spins on its axis, every part of it spends some time turned away from the sun's light and so plunged into darkness. The terminator is the boundary that slices the moon between bright day and shadowed night.

2 REFLECTED LIGHT

Just as moonlight illuminates nights on Earth, earthshine can brighten moon evenings. The sunlight that strikes Earth's daytime side is reflected onto the moon, and returns to us as a dim glow.

SPACE TRAVEL ATTRACTIONS

MUST-SEE

Visit the Apollo 11 lunar module landing site, where U.S. astronaut Neil Armstrong became the first person ever to step on another space object on July 20, 1969.

GET A JUMP ON THINGS

Grab a pogo stick and lift off. In the moon's low-gravity environment a typical bounce could thrust you six feet (1.8 m) high.

VIEW THE HORIZON'S GLOW

As you orbit the moon, catch the glow of dust grains propelled more than 62 miles (100 km) high by static charges. Sunlight reflecting off the grains makes the horizon seem to glow.

MOONSCAPE
A battered surface of craters and PLAINS

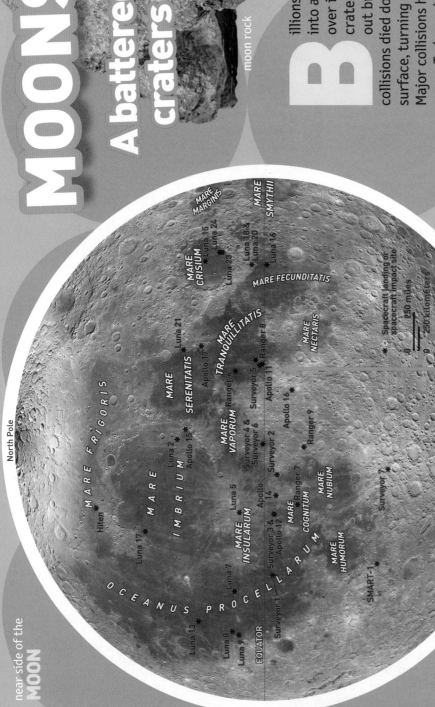

near side of the
MOON

North Pole

MARE MARGINIS
MARE SMYTHII
MARE CRISIUM
Luna 15
Luna 24
Luna 18 &
Luna 20
Luna 16
MARE FECUNDITATIS
Luna 23
Luna 21
MARE SERENITATIS
Apollo 17
MARE TRANQUILLITATIS
Ranger 6
Surveyor 5
Ranger 8
Apollo 11
MARE NECTARIS
Apollo 16
Ranger 9
MARE VAPORUM
Surveyor 4 &
Surveyor 6
Surveyor 2
Ranger 7
Apollo 15
Luna 2
Apollo 14
Apollo 12
Luna 5
Surveyor 3 &
Surveyor 1
MARE INSULARUM
MARE COGNITUM
MARE NUBIUM
MARE HUMORUM
Luna 7
Luna 8
Luna 9
Luna 17
Hiten
MARE FRIGORIS
MARE IMBRIUM
OCEANUS PROCELLARUM
EQUATOR
SMART-1
Surveyor 7
Lunar Prospector
LCROSS/
Centaur Impactor
Chandrayaan-1
Moon Impact
Probe
South Pole
Selene/
Kaguya
Spacecraft landing or
spacecraft impact site

0   250 miles
0   250 kilometers

moon rock

Billions of years ago, space objects crashed into a young moon and left their marks all over its surface. They scooped out huge craters, raised mountains, and hollowed out broad but shallow basins. After the collisions died down, micrometeorites pummeled the surface, turning the surface rock into a fine powder. Major collisions have stopped, but all is not quiet on the moon. Today, scientific instruments reveal that it is bombarded by solar wind and cosmic rays, and micrometeorites still hit the surface.

On moon maps, many features are given Latin names. *Mare* is an impact crater covered with lava. Oceanus Procellarum, "Ocean of Storms," is an enormous mare. Astronaut landings were all Apollo missions.

COOL FACTS TO RECORD

1. SMOOTH SEAS
Lava-filled basins

Some objects that hit the moon caused the lunar crust to split open. Lava then oozed up, flowed into enormous impact basins, and hardened into smooth, dark surfaces. This process formed what we now call the lunar maria (from *mare*, the Latin word for "seas"). This kind of ground made for a safe landing site for Apollo 11, which landed at the Sea of Tranquility (Mare Tranquillitatis).

far side of the
MOON

2 SOLID AS A ROCK?

It was long thought that the moon was solid rock but it may be hiding some liquid layers beneath its crust. The thick mantle seems soft, possibly molten. It surrounds an iron core that may be partially liquid.

crust
mantle
outer core
inner core

3 MAPPING THE FAR SIDE
Lunar pics

We rely on robotic spacecraft to map the face of the moon that is never visible from Earth—the far side. In 1959 the Soviet Luna 3 spacecraft shot and developed the first photograph before sending a scan to Earth.

4 ASTRONOMICAL FORCES
Moon mountains

Lunar mountains may have formed when comets and asteroids slammed into the moon. In these lunar smashups, gaping holes opened and lunar rock was forced upward. In only minutes, one-mile (1.6-km)-high mountain peaks towered above new craters.

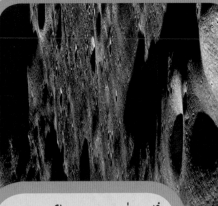

INNER SOLAR SYSTEM

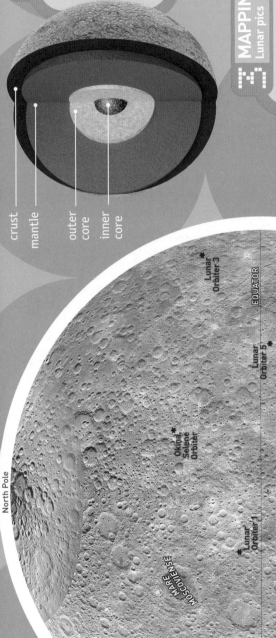

North Pole

MARE MOSCOVIENSE

Okina Selene Orbiter

Lunar Orbiter 1

Lunar Orbiter 3

Lunar Orbiter 5

Ranger 4

EQUATOR

MARE ORIENTALE

MARE INGENII

* Spacecraft landing or spacecraft impact site

Lunar Orbiter 2

MARE AUSTRALE

South Pole

0   250 miles
0   250 kilometers

South Pole–Aitkin basin

5 RECORD BREAKER
Giant impact crater

The South Pole–Aitkin basin—the cratered area at the top in this colorized image—holds two records. About half the width of the United States, it is the largest impact feature on the moon. It is also the first place where lunar water ice was discovered.

EXPLORING THE MOON

Establishing the next FRONTIERS

model of a spacecraft that may be used to study the moon's atmosphere

DID YOU KNOW?

Scientists have created artificial moon surfaces with boulders and molded craters. They use these pretend landscapes to test and challenge model moon rovers.

The moon is likely to be the first stop for future space pioneers. From moon bases, astronauts might prepare launch sites and vehicles for adventures deep into space. Of course, at the bases astronauts won't see a moon in their sky, passing through phases such as crescent and full moon (see pages 10–11). Instead, they will see Earth going through its own sequence of phases as different parts of it are lit by the sun. The sight will reinforce the close connection of the moon, Earth, and sun.

SPACE TRAVEL ATTRACTIONS

FOUR-WHEELING IN SPACE
Recharge the battery of a 1970s Apollo moon buggy left behind decades ago. After all that exposure in the lunar environment, will the buggy still run?

DIG IT
Take a lunar mine tour. Colonists will likely mine the moon for vital resources, such as the water frozen in the surface and oxygen in the molecules of soil minerals.

TAKE IN THE VIEW
Relive the Apollo astronauts' amazing experiences. Trek across the lunar surface, be awestruck by huge craters, and enjoy watching Earth rise above the horizon.

5 FAR SIDE RADIO

Free from radio interference from Earth, the far side of the moon would make a great location for catching extraterrestrial radio vibes. In the future, a radio telescope might be built on the far side.

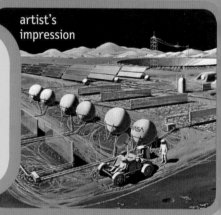

artist's impression

4 ROBOT SCIENCE

Rovers help us with continued exploration of the moon. China's Yutu rover recently helped discover a type of moon rock that may be three billion years old.

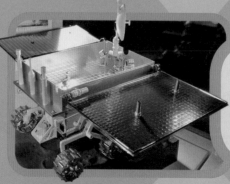

5 COOL FACTS TO RECORD

TIME TRAVELER!
Sometime in the next 20 to 30 years, you might be able to get to the moon by lunar elevator. After transferring to the elevator car in Earth's orbit, you'll travel the equivalent of 5.7 million floors to the lunar surface. Your ride should take about six months.

1 MOON MEET-UP

In 1969, U.S. astronaut Alan Bean captured this picture of fellow crewman Charles Conrad, Jr., with the lander Surveyor, which had touched down 18 months earlier. This was the first and so far only time that people stood near a lander sent before them to another space object. (In the background is the astronauts' Apollo 12 lander.)

INNER SOLAR SYSTEM

artist's impression

2 PREPARE FOR LANDING

The first stages of a lunar outpost might be built by robots sent from Earth. The robots could be used to get a head start, perhaps constructing the landing pad and domed living quarters like these for the first human visitors in more than 50 years.

3 MOONBASE ONE
A home site

High crater ridges at the moon's poles are likely to be the sites of the first lunar habitats because they provide three vital resources. These exposed sites receive solar energy for long periods. The constantly dark crater floors that are nearby are cold enough to keep water ice from evaporating. And minerals in the soil can be processed for oxygen.

an artist's depiction from the future, of astronauts watching Earth as it eclipses the sun

MARS
The red PLANET

Red is the color of blood, war, fire—and of Mars, the fourth planet from the sun. Slipping across the black, diamond-speckled sky, this ruby-colored planet seems like a warning light. In science fiction, we hear of Martian invasions. But it is Earthlings who are invading Mars! Landers, satellites, and spying flyby craft probe our mysterious neighbor's surface and atmosphere. They have revealed a varied landscape scoured by enormous dust devils and storms, our solar system's largest known canyon and impact crater, and evidence of a once watery world.

MARS DATA

Orbital period: 687 Earth days
Rotational period: 24.6 Earth hours
Diameter: 4,222 miles (6,794 km)
Mass: 0.1 Earth's
Density (water=1): 3.9
Gravity: 0.38 Earth's
Average distance from sun:
 141.6 million miles (227.9 million km)
Surface temperature: −125°F (−87°C)
 to 23°F (−5°C)
Moons: two

Earth   Mars

5 COOL FACTS TO RECORD

1. TECHNICAL ODYSSEY

The orbiter called 2001 Mars Odyssey was equipped with a thermal imager, a gamma-ray spectrometer, and a radiation detection system. These scientific instruments have revealed the chemical composition of Mars's soil and the potential dangers of the Martian environment to future human visitors.

SPACE TRAVEL ATTRACTIONS

➤ A MARTIAN SNOW SCENE
The magic of a Martian snowfall awaits you during each hemisphere's winter. You can even experience carbon dioxide snow, something you won't find on Earth.

➤ VALLES MARINERIS
Mind the gap! Dropping a dizzying 4.3 miles (7 km) from the edges of this gap—nearly twice the average depth of Earth's oceans—the 2,500-mile (about 4,000-km)-long chasm in the Martian crust is the largest known canyon system in the entire solar system.

➤ OLYMPUS MONS
Climb this majestic volcanic mountain. It juts 16 miles (25.7 km) into the Martian sky and spans an area the size of the state of Arizona, U.S.A. A sheer rock wall four miles (6.4 km) high gives way to 25-million-year-old lava fields that lead up to the top. This is our solar system's highest peak.

DIGITAL TRAVELER!
Enjoy a whirlwind experience from the comfort of your digital device. Search the Internet for "Martian dust devils NASA video" and select from simulations, time-lapse surface images, and videos that capture Martian dust devils in action.

4 DUST DEVILS

Windblown sands appear to dance across the planet's surface. Occasionally, plumes of dust one mile (1.6 km) high twirl like tornadoes (above) over Mars, leaving behind dark tracks of newly exposed soil.

5 MOONS AND ASTEROIDS

The Martian moons, Phobos and Deimos, travel with Mars in its orbit around the sun. They are joined by groups of asteroids known as Trojans, which are named after an army in Greek myths. The Trojans orbit the sun (not the planet), following Mars's path. Combined, the moons and asteroids measure less than one-millionth the size of Earth's moon.

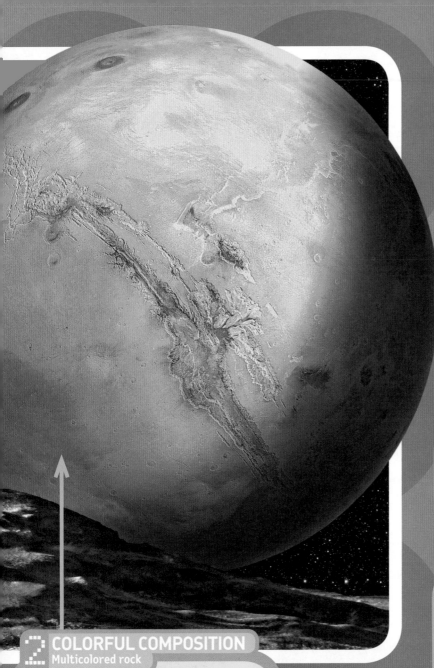

Deimos

Phobos

2 COLORFUL COMPOSITION
Multicolored rock

Close up, Mars looks like a multicolored mosaic, displaying shades of red, orange, tan, and yellow that look like they were applied to the planet's surface by a painter's brush. The colors are the work of chemistry, as iron in Mars rock combines with oxygen in the atmosphere to form rust. Oxygen—our life-sustaining substance—also exists on Mars.

An artist's concept of Mars seen from the surface of its largest moon, Phobos. It uses an actual Mars photo.

3 VIKINGS INVADE

Mars landers give us close-up, human-size glimpses of a world that looks familiar and yet so strange. On July 30, 1976, Viking 1 became the first lander to safely touch the surface and begin a fully successful mission. Its identical twin, Viking 2, soon followed.

MAPPING MARS
Exploration and
DISCOVERY

surface of
Mars

For many thousands of years, the face of Mars appeared as just a red point of light marching across the starry sky. Since 1960, space scientists have sent more than 20 orbiters, 7 landers, 5 rovers, and 13 probes to study Mars. (For details of these vehicles, see pages 140–141.) With technology like this, scientists have mapped Mars's mighty volcanoes, craters large and small, bright white ice caps, and wandering gorges. They have also established that, like Earth, Mars has a constantly changing surface.

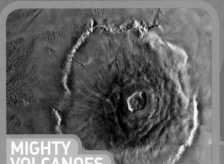

1 MIGHTY VOLCANOES
Olympus Mons

Mars has many striking volcanoes. Some are called paterae and are wide and low. Olympus Mons, the highest point on Mars, is 388 miles (624 km) across and 69,844 feet (21,288 m) high. It shows evidence of an explosive eruption from about three billion years ago.

DID YOU KNOW?

The 2015 movie, *The Martian*, was filmed in part in Wadi Rum, a desert area in the south of Jordan. After filming, the desert's vegetation had to be edited out of the shots to make it closely resemble a Martian landscape.

west side of
MARS

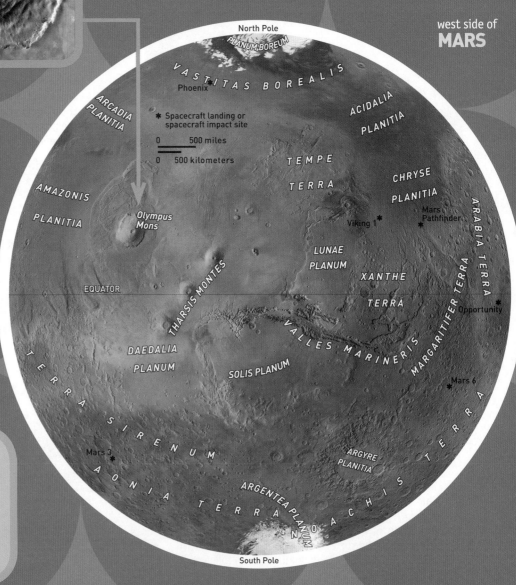

North Pole
PLANUM BOREUM
VASTITAS BOREALIS
Phoenix
ARCADIA PLANITIA
ACIDALIA PLANITIA
✳ Spacecraft landing or spacecraft impact site
0   500 miles
0   500 kilometers
TEMPE TERRA
CHRYSE PLANITIA
AMAZONIS PLANITIA
Olympus Mons
Viking 1 ✳
Mars Pathfinder ✳
ARABIA TERRA
LUNAE PLANUM
EQUATOR
XANTHE TERRA
THARSIS MONTES
VALLES MARINERIS
MARGARITIFER TERRA
Opportunity ✳
DAEDALIA PLANUM
SOLIS PLANUM
Mars 6 ✳
TERRA SIRENUM
Mars 3 ✳
ARGYRE PLANITIA
ARGENTEA PLANUM
AONIA TERRA
NOACHIS TERRA
PLANUM
South Pole

5 COOL FACTS TO RECORD

3 SECTION OF MARS

Scientists think that Mars has three layers. A thin, iron-rich, rocky crust tops a middle layer called the mantle. The mantle's main component is the element silicon. The innermost core is rich in iron, nickel, and possibly sulfur. The core may be a cooled, solid mass, or a hot, liquid mix.

crust
mantle
core

2 POLAR AVALANCHE
North Pole

On February 19, 2008, an avalanche in Mars's north polar region crashed down a 2,300-foot (701-m) cliff (above left) and kicked up a cloud of fine-grained ice and dust (on the right). This image of the billowing debris led to the first discovery of Martian avalanches.

4 IMPACT CRATERS

The scars of collisions with asteroids dot the surface of Mars, as seen here. Impact crater Utopia, at about 1,500 miles (2,414 km) wide, is probably the largest in the solar system.

east side of MARS

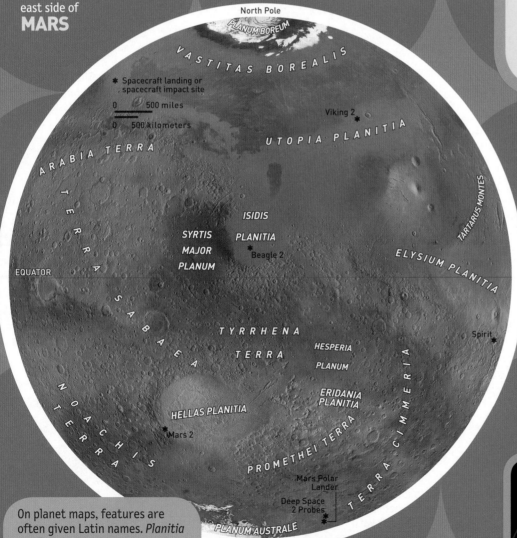

North Pole

PLANUM BOREUM

VASTITAS BOREALIS

* Spacecraft landing or spacecraft impact site

0   500 miles
0   500 kilometers

ARABIA TERRA

Viking 2 *

UTOPIA PLANITIA

TERRA

ISIDIS
PLANITIA

SYRTIS
MAJOR
PLANUM

Beagle 2 *

TARTARUS MONTES

ELYSIUM PLANITIA

EQUATOR

SABAEA

TYRRHENA
TERRA

HESPERIA
PLANUM

Spirit *

NOACHIS
TERRA

HELLAS PLANITIA

Mars 2 *

ERIDANIA
PLANITIA

PROMETHEI TERRA

TERRA CIMMERIA

Mars Polar
Lander
Deep Space
2 Probes *

PLANUM AUSTRALE

South Pole

On planet maps, features are often given Latin names. *Planitia* is a flat area within an impact site, *terra* a large landmass, and *vastitas* is a vast plain.

5 DUST STORMS

Wind whips dust from the Martian surface into the air, creating dust storms. Small storms last for a few hours, but massive clouds can churn for weeks and cover the planet.

63

LIFE ON MARS?

Past, present, and FUTURE

Curiosity rover research vehicle

L ife on Mars. The thought stirs something deep within our hearts and minds. Did life ever exist on this planet? Might it be there today, in the soil beneath the rovers' wheels? Early space scientists looked for signs of life and water that might sustain it over time. Mars missions have revealed water ice, flowing water, ancient seas, and—just perhaps—microbe fossils. We may yet find rare substances on Mars that could be key to discovering life on the planet.

SPACE TRAVEL ATTRACTIONS

→ **BLUE SUNRISES AND SUNSETS**
Dust in the Martian atmosphere absorbs and scatters blue light, producing a strange blue glow early in the mornings and evenings.

→ **MARVELOUS MOON DANCE**
From the surface, watch Mars's moon, Phobos, lap the planet three times in a single sol, the name for a Martian day.

→ **TRACK THE ROVERS**
For fun, follow the 35.2 miles (56.7 km) of rover wheel tracks created so far—if sand hasn't covered them yet.

5 COOL FACTS TO RECORD

1 ROCK FANS

Just as rivers on Earth drop deposits at their mouths in distinctive fan shapes, so did the flowing water on Mars in what is now the giant Valles Marineris (Mariner Valley). Slowly, over millions of years, the sediment here hardened to rock. Billions of years later, Mars missions reveal the riverbed cast in stone.

2 PROSPECTS FOR LIFE

Scientists looking for extraterrestrial life follow the water. The dark streaks in this colorized image show chemical signs of water. Because the streaks grow and shrink with the seasons, as do rivers on Earth, scientists think they may have found flowing water on present-day Mars.

A giant space hotel orbits Mars in this vision of the future.

3 TIGHT QUARTERS

In the 2020s, people may be on their way to Mars, propelled by a bigger, more efficient version of the rockets that blasted astronauts to the moon. The Orion Space Capsule will serve as bedroom, kitchen, bathroom, living room, lab, and office for six people, for six months—all in a space that's smaller than a typical classroom!

4 A MARTIAN HOME

An ideal habitat on Mars would protect people from the harsh environment and be made from resources found on the red planet. How would we make all that happen? One idea is to use a 3-D printer to shape Martian ice into sets of nesting shells like the one shown here. The thick ice layers would absorb dangerous radiation, yet let in light. Another idea is to bury living quarters into Martial soil, to shield the crew from the sun's radiation and to keep temperatures inside constant.

5 VITAL SIGNS

A Mars meteorite that fell to Earth 13,000 years ago contains certain molecules and minerals that might be signs of life. The substances were found clustered near tiny structures in the meteorite. These structures could be fossils or microbes.

DID YOU KNOW?

Some scientists speculate that chemical reactions on Mars were the beginning for all life on Earth. They think a basic start-up molecule for life, RNA (ribonucleic acid), formed on Mars, then soared to Earth inside Martian asteroids.

ASTEROID DATA

Orbital period: varies, but for most, 3 to 6 Earth years
Rotational period: varies from a couple of hours to many days
Diameter: from dust-size to 339 miles (545 km)
Mass: varies, most massive is 0.00004 Earth's
Density (water=1): varies, 1.38 to 5.32
Gravity: varies
Average distance from sun: 195.3 million miles (314.3 million km) to 306.9 million miles (493.9 million km)
Surface temperature: −100°F (−73.3°C)
Moons: some asteroids have moons

Earth   Ceres

5 COOL FACTS TO RECORD

5 SO GOOD TO SEE YOU

The first spacecraft to cruise into or beyond the asteroid belt, Pioneer 10, zoomed through on its way to Jupiter but did not stop to "look" around. Since then, spacecraft have visited 11 asteroids. The Galileo spacecraft provided the first close-up picture of the asteroid Gaspra (shown here).

Drifting past huge asteroids, a future spacecraft is shown circling the dwarf planet Ceres.

4 AND MILLIONS MORE

If you gathered and merged Ceres, Pallas, Vesta, the million other asteroids that each measure more than a few city blocks, and the countless smaller asteroids, the whole pile would still be smaller than Earth's moon.

AMONG THE ASTEROIDS

Rocky RUBBLE

1 CERES
Big, round, first

Claiming one-quarter of the asteroid belt's mass, Ceres is the largest and roundest object in this zone. Although it has been called a planet and an asteroid, it's now considered a dwarf planet—the first one studied by an orbiter.

2 BIG, OLD PALLAS

When its bigger relative Ceres was reclassified as a dwarf planet in 2006, Pallas became the largest asteroid—for now. Its composition suggests that Pallas is also one of the oldest objects in our solar system. In this illustration, Pallas has been struck on its underside by an asteroid.

Snowman

mountains

3 RECORD-BREAKING VESTA

More massive but slightly smaller than Pallas, Vesta averages about 300 miles (482 km) across. Although puny compared to a planet, it boasts one of the solar system's highest mountains—a 16-mile (26-km)-high peak seen here at the bottom of the image. The three craters (top left) are nicknamed "Snowman" because they form the shape of the wintry figure.

Welcome to the asteroid belt, an orbiting band of some of our solar system's first solid bits and pieces. It is also home to a larger space object, the dwarf planet Ceres. Asteroids vary in shape, size, and materials, but all are rocky and quite small compared to planets. These chunks never formed a planet. Many asteroids were ejected from the belt, often colliding with inner planets, making craters, doing damage, and sometimes offering up a shooting star on Earth, a bit of ancient rock burning as it streaks across a night sky.

SPACE TRAVEL ATTRACTIONS

APPRECIATE ASTEROID "RAIN"

Asteroids may be raining down around you right now. An estimated 100 tons (90 t) of minimeteorites fall to Earth each day. Some collectors gather the minimeteorites by dragging magnets along the ground, often near downspouts, because rain washes these tiny space treasures off rooftops.

GO MOON HOPPING

Visit the moons of more than 150 asteroids that are known to have their own natural satellites—rocks orbiting rocks!

QUENCH YOUR THIRST

Stop by Ceres for a drink. If Ceres turns out to have as much water as scientists think it might, there would be more freshwater on the dwarf planet than on Earth.

SPINNING WORLDS

Hurtling through SPACE

Asteroids hurtle toward Earth—an imaginary scene

A steroids are some of the oldest objects in the solar system. So they can shed light on the solar system's distant past. Rich with metals and possibly water, some asteroids are roaming resource treasure troves. Perhaps they'll support space colonies and industry on Earth. Other asteroids may be dangerous to our home planet, with the potential to collide with Earth. Scientists are watching them and learning how to nudge them out of our way.

SPACE TRAVEL ATTRACTIONS

➤ TAKE A ROCK FOR A SPIN AND TWIST

Some small asteroids rotate once every few minutes. Hop on one and you might experience sunrise and sunset 480 times in 24 hours.

➤ CLAIM IT, NAME IT

Keep your eyes peeled to discover an asteroid. The people in charge of asteroid naming rules, the International Astronomical Union's Committee on Small Body Nomenclature, are pretty easygoing, so you can name your asteroid (almost) anything you want.

➤ GO BEYOND THE BELT

Leave the belt to see other inner solar system asteroids. Check out near-Earth asteroids, whose orbits pass near Earth's. Visit a Trojan asteroid. Locked in a sweet spot of balanced gravity between the sun and a planet, a Trojan asteroid always leads or trails that planet in its track around the sun.

2. HEDGEHOG ROVERS

In the future, a small, manned vehicle will leave a space station to approach an asteroid. It will release "hedgehogs" onto the surface. These nubby cubes (one shown here in this artist's impression) will bounce, roll, and make their own tornado effects to spin themselves out of sand before roving across the asteroid.

---

5 COOL FACTS TO RECORD

1. ANCIENT METEORITES

Sometime before Earth's formation, asteroid Vesta smashed into another body. The impact scattered chunks that eventually landed on Earth. Five percent of all of our planet's meteorites are thought to be pieces of Vesta.

CAN WE DIG IT?
Mining asteroids

Near-Earth asteroids contain natural resources, including water and various metals. Space experts envision mining these resources in the future to support space exploration and colonization—for example, using water to drink or process into oxygen or fuel.

DID YOU KNOW?

Every day, small meteorites land on Earth, but really big ones are extremely rare. The record-holder is the Hoba meteorite, about as wide as a tour bus and as heavy as 10 adult elephants.

an illustration of what it might be like to mine an asteroid in the future

EARTH CROSSERS!

In 2012, an asteroid about half the size of a basketball court plummeted through Earth's atmosphere and broke apart between 12 and 15 miles (19 and 24 km) above the ground. The blast was felt for hundreds of miles (km). Although no known near-Earth objects pose any threat within the next 100 years, scientists track them—just in case.

NOT-SO-CLOSE ENCOUNTER

The asteroid belt contains lots of rocks but it's not too crowded. The closest encounter between Pioneer 10—the first spacecraft to cross this zone—and a large meteor was one million miles (1,609,344 km). That's like a fruit fly navigating between New York City's Statue of Liberty and Big Ben, in London, England.

69

AUNT BERTHA'S SPACE TRAVEL TIPS

Binoculars help when you want to spy planets of the outer solar system. An astronomy club's telescope and members are a great bonus.

Any radio communications between the outer solar system and Earth are delayed. From Jupiter, plan on it taking about two hours to say, "Hello!" to someone on Earth and get a response. From the outermost regions, plan on at least two years.

No need to pack many shoes. The planets here are all made of gas, so you won't be walking—much. Bring moon boots, though! You'll visit lots of moons.

OUTER SOLAR SYSTEM

Home to giants, comets, and DWARFS

Beyond the asteroid belt, vast expanses separate enormous planets, which are many times the size of Earth. As a comparison, if Earth were the size of a marble, Jupiter would be a basketball, Saturn a soccer ball, Uranus a softball, and Neptune a baseball. Past the planets, distances stretch on, but the solar system objects become smaller. Here you will find cousins to Ceres—the other dwarf planets— and more asteroids. You'll also encounter comets—the ultimate travelers of the whole system. Sometimes spectacular as they whip around the sun, comets emerge from far beyond the planets' orbits. Some come from the farthest reaches of the mighty sun's gravitational influence. Follow them outward, toward the solar system's edge.

Bringing people to and through the outer solar system will likely require new propulsion systems. There are no plans right now for human missions beyond Mars—only vivid dreams like this space trading craft drifting in orbit around Jupiter.

GIANT JUPITER

A planet made of GAS

Jupiter

Earth

Beyond the asteroid belt, Jupiter rules! Not just "big," it outsizes all other solar system planets combined. Not merely "giant," it possesses outer layers heavy enough to squeeze the hydrogen below them into one of the most compressed forms possible, liquid metallic hydrogen. Mighty Jupiter's gravity affected the distribution of asteroids in the belt—from more than 200 million miles (322 million km) away. Of all the planets in the solar system, its daily rotation is the swiftest, and its magnetic field is the strongest. Some of Jupiter's moons are pretty remarkable, too.

SPACE TRAVEL ATTRACTIONS

BRIGHT LIGHTS
Catch the special effects in Jupiter's outer cloud layers as they brighten with lightning. The flashes can be 1,000 times more powerful than any on Earth. In addition, spiral-shaped auroras shimmer when "seen" with ultraviolet and X-ray detectors.

CHEMICAL SNOWFALL
Bundle up! Between Jupiter's two highest cloud layers, temperatures hover at around −234°F (−148°C). Icy droplets of ammonia form in the white ammonia clouds that we see as part of the shifting patterns in Jupiter's stripes. This ammonia snow falls down to the reddish ammonium hydrosulfide gas cloud layer below.

A TRUE HEAVYWEIGHT
At the tops of Jupiter's clouds, gravity pulls twice as hard as it does on Earth's surface. There, a gallon (3.8 L) container of milk will feel like it is filled with granite, and an average high schooler will weigh more than an Earth-based NFL lineman.

5 GIVE ME A RING (OR THREE)

In addition to 67 moons, Jupiter has three rings! Nestled about halfway between Jupiter and its moon Io, they were discovered in 1979 during the U.S. Voyager 1 mission. These thin bands are made of dust flung into Jupiter's orbit when micrometeorites crash into the small inner moons.

4 STRIPES AND SWIRLS

Jupiter's swift rotation acts like an artist's hand, setting powerful winds in motion, up to 400 miles an hour (644 km/h). The winds are the brush that pulls clouds of multicolored gas into bands, while more gases well up from below.

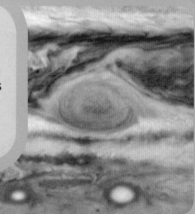

1 SEEING RED

Long before you or even your grandparents were born, the astronomer Giovanni Domenico Cassini (1625–1712) recorded a spot on Jupiter—a storm that is likely the same Great Red Spot we see today. It has definitely been tracked since the 1830s. Wide enough to fit two Earths side by side, this spot is a giant, raging hurricane, and the solar system's strongest known storm. Here, an imagined future spacecraft flies over the spot.

5 COOL FACTS TO RECORD

2 THE GIANT'S FORCE FIELD

A strong magnetic field surrounds Jupiter. It is thought to originate from the rapidly spinning, rare substance, liquid metallic hydrogen, which is found deep within the planet. Jupiter's magnetism is about 18,000 times the strength of Earth's. Warped by its interaction with the solar wind, this magnetic field stretches all the way out to Saturn.

3 WHAT LIES BENEATH?

Dark lines crisscross the icy crust of Europa, one of Jupiter's moons. Scientists think the colored material has emerged through cracks in its icy surface. These fractures are one sign of a suspected salty ocean—one that could support life.

an imaginary view of gas giant Jupiter as seen from the frozen surface of Europa

73

JUPITER AND ITS MOONS

A huge planet with orbiting MOONS

surface of Europa, one of the moons of Jupiter

Up until Galileo Galilei aimed his telescope at Jupiter in 1609, no one suspected it was so much like Earth—a sphere with features on it and even its own moons. Seeing Jupiter's orbiting moons challenged the idea of the time that everything revolved around Earth. Today, we know more about our solar system and about Jupiter. It is a giant cloud of gas, and if it had been bigger when it formed, it may have ignited deep inside and become a star instead of a planet. We also have discovered a total of 67 moons. But the moons Galileo discovered—Europa, Callisto, Io, and Ganymede—still offer mysteries.

2 DELVING INTO JUPITER

Instruments aboard the U.S. Juno spacecraft, which entered Jupiter's orbit in July 2016, can help explore Jupiter's interior, including its suspected solid core and its layer of liquid metallic hydrogen, the rare form of matter that is thought to be a key ingredient for Jupiter's powerful magnetic field.

1 TAKE THE PLUNGE

Below Jupiter's frigid upper cloud layer is about 600 miles (966 km) of increasingly dense atmosphere followed by a 12,000-mile (19,312-km)-deep layer of liquid hydrogen. Under that is an ocean of thick liquid metallic hydrogen, which may give way to a solid, rocky core.

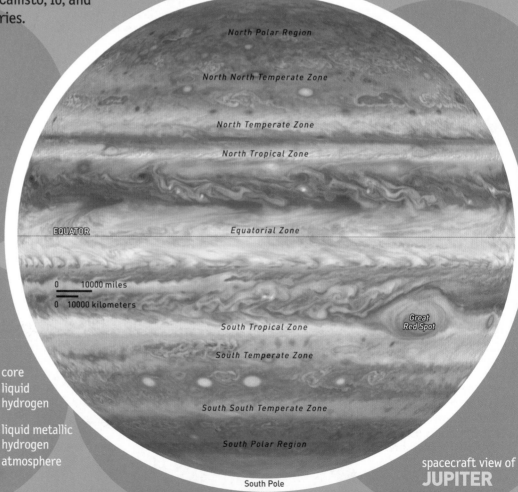

North Pole

North Polar Region

North North Temperate Zone

North Temperate Zone

North Tropical Zone

EQUATOR — Equatorial Zone

0   10000 miles
0   10000 kilometers

South Tropical Zone

Great Red Spot

South Temperate Zone

South South Temperate Zone

South Polar Region

South Pole

core
liquid hydrogen
liquid metallic hydrogen
atmosphere

spacecraft view of **JUPITER**

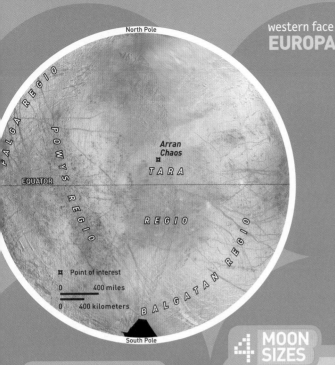

western face of
EUROPA

North Pole

FALGA REGIO

POWYS REGIO

Arran
Chaos ⊡

TARA

REGIO

Equator

BALGATAN REGIO

⊡ Point of interest

0 — 400 miles

0 — 400 kilometers

South Pole

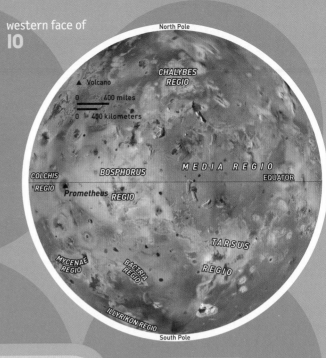

western face of
IO

North Pole

▲ Volcano

0 — 400 miles

0 — 400 kilometers

CHALYBES REGIO

COLCHIS REGIO

BOSPHORUS

MEDIA REGIO

Equator

Prometheus REGIO

MYCENAE REGIO

BACTRIA REGIO

TARSUS

REGIO

ILLYRIKON REGIO

South Pole

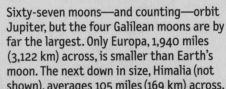

4 MOON SIZES

Sixty-seven moons—and counting—orbit Jupiter, but the four Galilean moons are by far the largest. Only Europa, 1,940 miles (3,122 km) across, is smaller than Earth's moon. The next down in size, Himalia (not shown), averages 105 miles (169 km) across.

3 EUROPA AND CALLISTO

Europa is a promising site for finding life. Beneath its icy surface, it may be home to a saltwater ocean with a nutrient-rich rock floor. Life on Earth likely began in a similar environment. Callisto is distinct for having the solar system's most heavily cratered surface. But it shows little signs of any geologic activity in the past four billion years.

GALILEAN MOONS

MOON SCALE

Europa   Io   Callisto   Ganymede

MOON ORBITS

Callisto   Io   Europa

JUPITER   Ganymede

5 IO AND GANYMEDE

Swinging closely around Jupiter in its orbit, Io experiences intense gravitational forces—enough to make solid rock melt and lead to the highest volcanic activity in the solar system. Muted Ganymede, larger than Mercury, is the biggest moon in the solar system. With suspected layers of ice and salty water that might touch rock, it might support life.

OUTER SOLAR SYSTEM

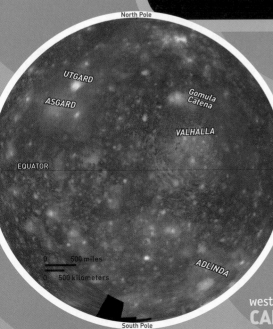

North Pole

UTGARD

ASGARD

Gomula
Catena

VALHALLA

Equator

500 miles

500 kilometers

ADLINDA

South Pole

western face of
CALLISTO

On moon maps, features are often given Latin names. *Catena* is chain of craters, *regio* a large, well-defined area, and *sulcus* a set of ridges or grooves.

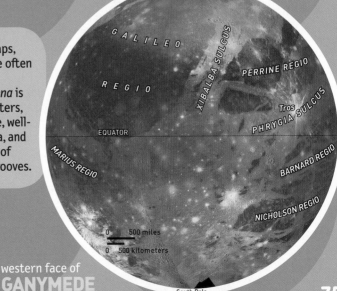

North Pole

GALILEO

XIBALBA SULCUS

REGIO

PERRINE REGIO

Tros

PHRYGIA SULCUS

Equator

MARIUS REGIO

BARNARD REGIO

NICHOLSON REGIO

500 miles

500 kilometers

South Pole

western face of
GANYMEDE

FUTURE JUPITER

Pushing forward with new TECHNOLOGIES

Jupiter is more than twice as far from Earth as Mars, yet people have sent several spacecraft to visit it. These missions have clued us in to the possibilities of warm, life-supporting oceans on some moons. They have shown that most of Jupiter's natural satellites are asteroids captured by its gravitational pull. The craft have also led scientists to new questions about how solar systems form. Improvements in space technology will make future journeys to Jupiter less expensive and allow probes to be packed with more scientific equipment. Take a look at what future expeditions to this gas giant might be like.

1 GROUNDED IN GOLDSTONE

One aim of the U.S. Juno mission to Jupiter is to precisely map the gravitational field of the planet. This can help scientists probe its internal structure. While in orbit around Jupiter, Juno will take measurements with the help of this radio antenna at Goldstone, California, U.S.A., that is part of the Deep Space Network system.

SPACE TRAVEL ATTRACTIONS

➥ SEE WHAT'S NEW
In 2000, three storms on Jupiter merged. The new combined spot, named Oval BA, was big—about half the size of the Great Red Spot, or one Earth wide. It started out white, but by 2005, its hue had changed twice, finally earning it the nickname "Red, Jr."

➥ WATCH A CLASSIC
Here on Earth, break out binoculars (or a telescope) to catch one or more eclipses of the Galilean moons while you wait for future missions to beam back amazing images of these space objects.

➥ GET A CHARGE OUT OF IO
Have you ever scuffed your feet along the carpet and given someone a slight shock? Similarly, as Io moves through Jupiter's magnetic field, electric energy builds and flows along Jupiter's magnetic lines. The energy discharges as giant lightning sparks in Jupiter's atmosphere, about 262,000 miles (421,650 km) away from Io.

2 INTO THE DEEP?

Astrobiologists hope one day there will be a mission to drill through Europa's 16-mile (26-km)-thick, icy crust to search for life in the salty ocean that is apparently underneath. In early design stages right now, ice-drilling, swimming, robotic "scientists" will do the job. Because the time delay between Earth and the outer planets prevents quick remote control, the robots must act and react—explore and "think"—independently.

artist's concept of Europa-based drilling machines mining the frozen moon's minerals

DID YOU KNOW?

To develop and test technologies that will help scientists explore distant destinations such as Europa, researchers send robots to remote places on Earth—such as the Andes mountains and Antarctica. As these missions test new technologies, they also advance scientific knowledge of Earth.

3 POWER UP

Electricity flows in a wire when it is moved through a magnetic field. That's the idea behind electrodynamic tethers—long electrical cables stretching from spacecraft as they orbit space objects with magnetic fields. These special tethers might be perfect for powering spacecraft at Jupiter and its moons, where magnetism is superstrong and sunlight for solar power is dim.

4 HOW PUSHY
Solar sail

Since the early 1900s, scientists have known that light gently pushes against matter. However, using this force for propulsion was science fiction—until Japan's IKAROS "light sail" demonstration helped take a craft past Venus in 2010. IKAROS is named for Interplanetary Kite-craft Accelerated by Radiation Of the Sun. Next up: a solar sailing mission to Jupiter's Trojan asteroids (see page 68).

(see page 68)

Possible future solar sail–powered craft drift through the vast distances of space.

5 DREAMING BIG

Right now, the dangers, technical challenges, and costs of a human voyage to Jupiter are still too great for space agencies to plan one. However, one scientist hopes to send a crew to Europa within the next 50 years, as envisioned here.

BEAUTIFUL SATURN

Surrounded by rings of dust and ICE

DID YOU KNOW?

As Earth and Saturn move through relatively tilted orbits, we see Saturn from different angles. Twice during Saturn's nearly 30-Earth-year orbit, we look at the rings edge-on, and they practically disappear. See more at *brunelleschi.imss.fi.it/esplora/cannocchiale* (click on Simulation, Astronomical discoveries, Saturn).

Its rings make Saturn famous—for good reason. They are one of the planet's most exciting and unique features. But there's more to enjoy about this planet, such as its soft colors and many moons. Its tremendous size is impressive. A single trip around Saturn's equator nearly matches the journey from Earth to the moon. Also, consider how far out in space it orbits. You could fit the entire radius of the inner solar system, from the sun to the outer edge of the asteroid belt, between Jupiter and Saturn. Meet Saturn, another mighty gas giant and the solar system's second largest planet.

DIGITAL TRAVELER!
"Listen" to Saturn radio! A sensor captured invisible signals (in the form of radio waves) that are closely related to the planet's auroras. A sound was assigned to each signal based on the characteristics of its energy. Tune in via the NASA website, searching for "sounds of Cassini."

SATURN DATA

Orbital period: 29.4 Earth years
Rotational period: 10.7 Earth hours
Diameter: 74,897 miles (120,535 km)
Mass: 95.2 Earth's
Density (water=1): 0.69
Gravity: 1.07 Earth's
Average distance from sun: 890.8 million miles (1,434 million km)
Surface temperature: −288°F (−178°C)
Moons: 62

Saturn

Earth

5 COOL FACTS TO RECORD

artist's impression of Saturn, seen from the surface of the moon Mimas

1 FROM YELLOW TO BLUE

Saturn's rings cast striped shadows across its northern hemisphere. In dimmer light, the usual, yellowish clouds cool and sink. Sunlight interacts differently with this clearer atmosphere, and we see blue. Meanwhile, in this scientific image, one of Saturn's moons, Mimas, appears as a crescent floating above the planet.

2 HEX MARKS THE SPOT

In 2004, scientists could not see what drives a unique, hexagonal (six-sided) cloud band near Saturn's north pole. It was Saturn's winter and the pole tipped into darkness. By 2013, springtime sunlight revealed a furious, hurricane-like polar storm multiple Earths wide (shown in this colorized image).

SPACE TRAVEL ATTRACTIONS

SKINNY RINGS

See for yourself how thin Saturn's rings are. Not counting the faintest, very-far-out G ring, their outermost diameter is nine million times their thickness. Picture it this way: If it were a 2.5-inch (6.4-cm)-high bagel, it would be wide enough to stretch across New Mexico.

WHIPPING WINDS

Catch Saturn's winds while they are still the fastest in the solar system. Some have reached 1,120 miles an hour (1,802 km/h), but they seem to be slowing. Now the mightiest winds measure "only" 895 miles an hour (1,440 km/h)—still more than three times faster than any wind on Earth.

LIGHT PACKER

Saturn is massive, but its overall size means it's not densely packed. Averaged out, one cup of Saturn would weigh less than one cup of water. Given a large enough pool, Saturn would float.

3 IN THE BANDS

Thanks to the latest studies, Saturn's stripes are clearer than ever before. Dark stripes in the atmosphere are thought to be where gases are rising from lower levels, and light-colored belts mark where gases are sinking. The motions of gases are part of Saturn's weather system.

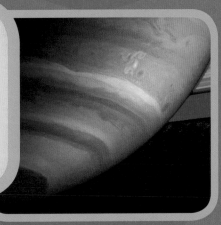

4 THE NITTY GRITTY ON DUST

This artist's image is based on data about dust around Saturn. Scientists track dust's movements for clues about how the rings form and change. Some of the dust seems to come from the space between stars. This dust is grainy, not icy (see pages 82–83), and was probably formed in the death of nearby stars.

5 STORMY WEATHER

Typically, Saturn's so-called Great White Spots are giant summer storms. Recently, however, a colossal one began in spring, eventually growing to two billion square miles (5.2 billion km²)— enough to cover Earth about 10 times. Thunder, lightning, and hail raged for 200 Earth days—about as long as a school year.

IN A SPIN

Saturn's multiple MOONS

A long with Saturn's rings, many moons orbit the planet. Sixty-two are identified, but scientists expect to discover more. Several, including far-flung Phoebe, orbit "backward"—in a direction opposite most of the pack. The moons have other differences, too. Titan, Rhea, Iapetus, Dione, Tethys, Enceladus, and Mimas are spherical, oval, or egglike, but all the other moons have irregular shapes. Titan and are especially interesting to scientists hoping to find life off Earth. Although they vary, they share something in common. Each moon holds valuable information that helps complete scientists' understanding of Saturn, our solar system, and the systems beyond.

Huygens probe on the surface of Titan

5 COOL FACTS TO RECORD

1. SATURN'S STRUCTURE

Gaseous layers of water ice, ammonia-rich substances, and ammonia crystals cover a liquid ocean of mostly hydrogen. Under this is a liquid metallic hydrogen layer, covering what is thought to be a rocky core.

2. ENCELADUS SPOUTS OFF

Impressive plumes of material erupt from at least 100 geysers on icy Enceladus. Some are hundreds of miles (km) high. Instead of lava, this moon spouts 194°F (90°C) hot water and substances that could be building blocks for life. This makes Enceladus one hot spot for seeking extra-terrestrial life.

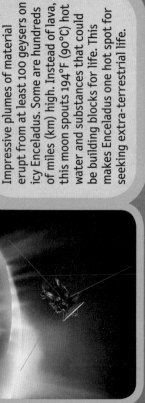

On the map, the zones and regions are movements of gases creating Saturn's weather (see page 79).

North Pole

North Polar Region

North North Temperate Zone

North Temperate Zone

North Tropical Zone

Equatorial Zone

South Tropical Zone

South Temperate Zone

South South Temperate Zone

South Polar Region

South Pole

EQUATOR

0   10000 miles

0   10000 kilometers

SATURN
based on NASA's Cassini mission images

western face of
ENCELADUS

Andal'Jus Sulci

Sind Sulci

Makran Sulci

EQUATOR

South Pole

0   50 miles
0   50 kilometers

On moon maps, features are often given Latin names. *Chasma* is a deep groove, *dorsa* a giant ridge, and *sulci* are sets of ridges and grooves.

western face of
TITAN

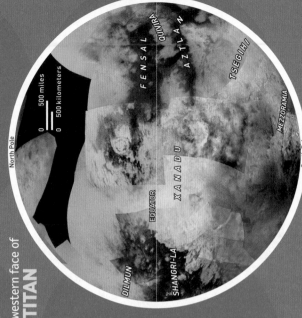

North Pole

FENSAL   QUIVIRA

AZTLAN

TSEGIHI

XANADU

EQUATOR

MEZZORAMIA

DILMUN

SHANGRI-LA

South Pole

0   500 miles
0   500 kilometers

western face of
MIMAS

:: PUZZLING
:: INTERIOR

Mimas's outsized Herschel crater is impressive, but planetologists are also interested in what's inside this moon. Its motion suggests a liquid ocean under the crust, but Mimas has been thought to be too cool for one. Another explanation: Mimas's core might be football-shaped.

western face of
DIONE

:: NOT QUITE
:: EARTH'S TWIN

Lakes. Dunes. Mountains. Precipitation. A thick, nitrogen-rich atmosphere. Like Earth, Titan has all of these features. However, the mountains are made of water ice, the lakes are filled with liquid hydrocarbons (substances containing hydrogen and carbon), and the sands are solid hydrocarbons that rain down from the clouds.

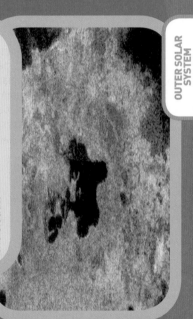

OUTER SOLAR
SYSTEM

EQUATOR

40 miles
40 kilometers

Camelot
Chasma

Herschel

Ossia Chasma

Avalon Chasma

South Pole

North Pole

:: SPUN
:: AROUND?

Although scientists expected otherwise, the back edge (western face) of Dione shows more signs of impacts than the front edge. Why? Perhaps an impactor made Dione spin exactly halfway around.

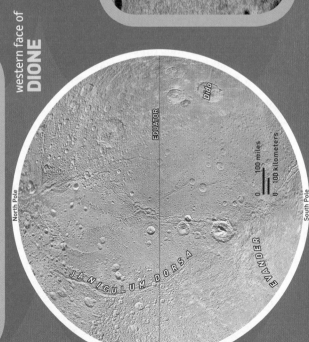

North Pole

EQUATOR

Dido

JANICULUM DORSA

EVANDER

South Pole

0   100 miles
0   100 kilometers

5 COOL FACTS TO RECORD

SPACE TRAVEL ATTRACTIONS

UNDER THE RING-BOW
Hover just above Saturn's equator for a unique view of the rings. They rise above you like an elongated rainbow or arch stretching between the horizons to the east and west.

RING DANCE
They may seem immovably rigid, but watch for the motion as bits and pieces in each ring respond to the gravity of moons, and the whole ring begins to ripple.

EYES ON THE (SNOW) BALL
From your ringside seat, see chunks of ice in Saturn's rings clumping up and forming odd-shaped "snowballs." Some grow to nearly the length of New York City's Manhattan Island.

1 THE DIRT ON THE RINGS

Special spacecraft sensors can detect energy signals from different types of materials. Then computers can make a map of where different materials are. When a computer assigned the color blue to icy particles and red to dust in Saturn's rings, scientists saw that the inner rings may be "dirtier" than the outer.

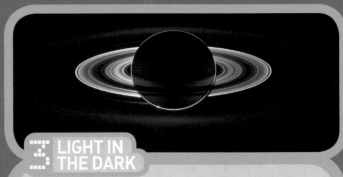

2 LEARN YOUR ABCs

Saturn's rings are named after the letters of the alphabet, in order of their discovery. From Saturn outward, look for them: D, C, B, A, F, G, and E. Of the nine moons discovered before the age of superior telescopes, three—Mimas, Encedalus, and Tethys—orbit between the G and E Rings. The other six (Dione, Rhea, Titan, Hyperion, Iapetus, and Phoebe) orbit way beyond all known rings. The Cassini Division is a unique giant gap between rings B and A.

3 LIGHT IN THE DARK

Seen with the sun blocked by Saturn, the planet's rings shine like delicate halos. Images like this Cassini photo, which is close to natural color, are awe-inspiring and reveal fine detail. For example, in shots from October 2006, researchers spotted two faint rings, never seen before.

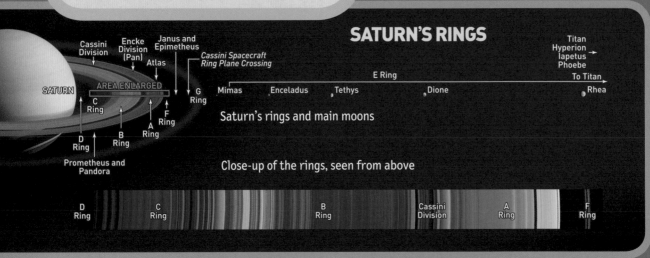

SATURN'S RINGS

Cassini Division
Encke Division (Pan)
Janus and Epimetheus
Atlas
Cassini Spacecraft Ring Plane Crossing

SATURN
AREA ENLARGED
C Ring
G Ring

Titan Hyperion Iapetus Phoebe

E Ring
To Titan

Mimas   Enceladus   Tethys   Dione   Rhea

D Ring
B Ring
A Ring
F Ring

Prometheus and Pandora

Saturn's rings and main moons

Close-up of the rings, seen from above

D Ring   C Ring   B Ring   Cassini Division   A Ring   F Ring

SATURN'S RINGS

Amazing orbiting FEATURES

Swing on over to Saturn's spectacular rings! Seen through low-powered telescopes, they look like bright but rigid bumps on either side of Saturn. With better equipment and missions to Saturn, their true nature has been revealed. The rings are made of bright, reflective bits and pieces of material—some dust and dirt, but mostly water ice. They are in constant, fluid motion as each piece orbits Saturn. The fragments are organized into rings with divisions between them—each ring is actually thousands of skinny ringlets with narrow gaps in between. What an amazing work of natural art!

DIGITAL TRAVELER
Take a sightseeing tour around Saturn via actual images from Cassini's approach to the planet. Board your virtual spaceship by visiting the NASA website and searching for "Cassini approaches Saturn."

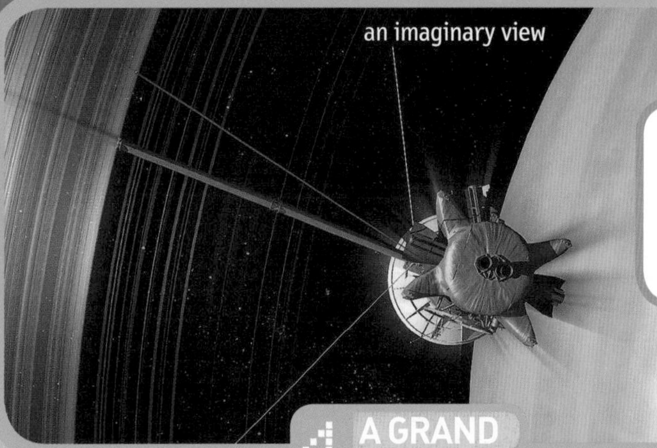

an imaginary view

OUTER SOLAR SYSTEM

4 A GRAND FINALE

Having remotely toured the Saturn system for 12 years, Cassini will start its final mission late in 2016. The Cassini Grand Finale includes 22 daredevil dives between the innermost rings and Saturn's upper atmosphere before a farewell plunge into the planet.

5 ROUNDING UP ROCKS

Like shepherds guiding the movements of sheep, so-called shepherd moons, such as Pandora and Prometheus, maintain the rings. As they orbit, their gravitational forces combine to keep particles and chunks within the rings' paths, as shown in this artist's impression.

Saturn

FROZEN URANUS
A world on a ROLL

blue-green Uranus

1 VIEW FROM DOWN-UNDER

The same 1986 Voyager 2 flyby of Uranus also was an opportunity to get close-up shots of moons Oberon (seen here), Ariel, Titania, Umbriel, and Miranda—but only their southern sides.

Barely visible to the human eye, Uranus—the seventh planet from the sun—was first known as a star. When its motion was discovered in 1781, it was briefly thought to be a comet. Taking up the space of about 63 Earths, Uranus is pretty big—but not like Jupiter or Saturn. It could fit inside Jupiter nearly 22 times, in Saturn, 13. Still, Uranus shares features with these two planets—a powerful magnetic field, no solid surface, high winds, rings, and multiple moons. Little explored, this blue-green sphere undoubtedly has other unique features yet to be discovered.

2 PLANET AT A GLANCE

Five and a half hours—about one school day. That's all the time scientists have spent up close to Uranus. On January 24, 1986, Voyager 2 sped past Uranus, as close as 50,000 miles (80,467 km). Scientists discovered 10 moons, two inner rings, a record cold planetary temperature, and Uranus's magnetic field.

SPACE TRAVEL ATTRACTIONS

❯ ROLL WITH IT
Tilted almost completely sideways, Uranus seems to roll along its orbit, more like a wheel on an axle than a spinning top. It is possible that a collision long ago walloped Uranus, toppling it sideways.

❯ GRAB SUNSCREEN AND A SUN LAMP
Uranus's extreme tilt means that in its summer, one hemisphere points nearly directly toward the sun. For 42 Earth years, the pole is in constant sunlight. In winter, when a hemisphere faces away from the sun, its pole is engulfed in darkness for another 42 Earth years.

❯ ENJOY A YEAR OF A LIFETIME
Think of an 84-year-old person. In his or her entire lifetime, Uranus has orbited just once around the sun.

URANUS DATA

Orbital period: 83.8 Earth years
Rotational period: 17.2 Earth hours
Diameter: 31,763 miles (51,118 km)
Mass: 14.5 Earth's
Density (water=1): 1.3
Gravity: 0.89 Earth's
Average distance from sun:
  1,785 million miles (2,873 million km)
Surface temperature: −357°F (−216°C)
Moons: 27

Uranus

Earth

3 GOING RETRO

Most planets spin east to west. However, like Venus, Uranus spins in a direction that's backward compared to the direction that Earth and the other planets spin. If the United States were on Uranus, Californians would see sunrise before New Yorkers—the exact opposite of what actually happens on Earth.

DID YOU KNOW?

Uranus burps! Maybe not literally—but scientists think it forms giant bubbles of methane gas deep under its surface. When its summer comes and warms the atmosphere, the bubbles rise to the top and are thought to show themselves as bright clouds.

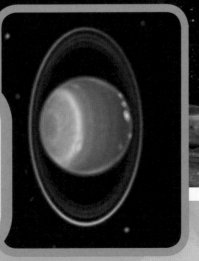

an artist's impression of Uranus and one of it moons seen from another moon, Miranda

4 FAMILIAR RING(S) TO IT

Like Jupiter and Saturn, Uranus has rings. Encircling its equator, all 13 appear vertical because of Uranus's extreme tilt. Earth telescopes helped make the first discovery of rings in 1977. In 1986, Voyager revealed additional rings. In 2003, the Hubble Space Telescope showed the 12th and 13th rings twice as far from the planet's surface as the others.

5 SHOWING ITS TRUE STRIPES

Methane gas, made of the chemical elements hydrogen and carbon, gives Uranus its aquamarine color. Clouds above the lower atmosphere layers obscure many details from view, but with various imaging technologies, scientists can see stripes. These are ultra-windy belts and zones, similar to what appears on Jupiter and Saturn.

1 A GIANT'S INTERIOR

Methane gives the blue-green tinge to Uranus's mainly helium and hydrogen atmosphere. Deeper, these gases mix with ices of water, ammonium, and stinky hydrogen sulphide. High pressure squeezes lower layers into denser, liquefied gas. This liquefied area may surround a central, dense core.

atmosphere

liquid mantle

core

URANUS
from Voyager 2 images

North Pole

Clouds

Atmospheric Color

EQUATOR

0   4000 miles

0   4000 kilometers

South Pole

2 SPOTTED DOTTED

Typically, auroras are major spectacles: showy curtains of light, often lasting for hours, days, or longer. Uranian auroras are short and spotty. Still, these dots of light in 2012 were a science thriller, because they were the first auroras seen on Uranus.

3 MIRANDA AND ARIEL

The home of the solar system's highest known cliff, Miranda is the smallest of Uranus's five round moons. Ariel, the brightest of the bunch, is crisscrossed by a vast system of valleys.

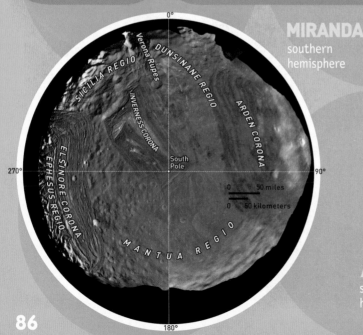

MIRANDA
southern hemisphere

0°

VERONA RUPES

SICILIA REGIO

DUNSINANE REGIO

INVERNESS CORONA

ARDEN CORONA

ELSINORE CORONA

EPHESUS REGIO

South Pole

270°

90°

0   50 miles

0   50 kilometers

MANTUA REGIO

180°

ARIEL
southern hemisphere

0°

Leprechaun Vallis

Brownie Chasma

KewPie Chasma

Kachina Chasmata

South Pole

270°

90°

0   100 miles

0   100 kilometers

180°

SPACE TRAVEL ATTRACTIONS

URANUS AND ITS MOONS

A variety of natural SATELLITES

THE THRILL OF THE CHILL

Uranus has the coldest temperature of all planets in the solar system. Scientists think this means it has no source of internal heating.

A STRANGE MAGNETISM

Three features make Uranus's magnetism odd. One: The magnetic poles are closer to Uranus's equator than to its geographical poles. Two: The line connecting the magnetic poles is far off the planet center. Three: The magnetism seems to be caused in a relatively shallow part of the planet.

CELEBRATE THE SOLSTICE

April 19, 2030—that's the day on Uranus when a narrow band north of the equator will receive its longest span of daylight of the Uranian year before nights grow longer and longer for 42 Earth years.

Swooping in their orbits around the blue, sideways-tipped Uranus, the planet's 27 known moons look from Earth like they are riding Ferris wheels instead of carousels. Before the space age launched in the late 1950s only five of the moons had been discovered—Miranda, Ariel, Umbriel, Titania, and Oberon. These are Uranus's only ball-shaped natural satellites. Each is roughly half ice, half rock. Yet, when Voyager 2 zoomed by and made partial portraits of the moons, each one showed its own character.

4 MISMATCHED MIRANDA

High ridges, plunging canyons, smooth ground, and more clash on Miranda's surface. Scientists once speculated that this mash-up was the result of the moon breaking apart and then rejoining. Now they think geological activity can explain the varied landscape.

On moon maps, features are often given Latin names. *Chasma* and *chasmata* are deep grooves, *corona* an oval area, *regio* a large landmass, and *rupes* is a cliff.

5 UMBRIEL AND TITANIA

Midsize Umbriel has a bright ring on its surface—perhaps frost. On Titania, the largest of Uranus's moons, giant troughs suggest that at some point the surface cracked open.

UMBRIEL
southern hemisphere

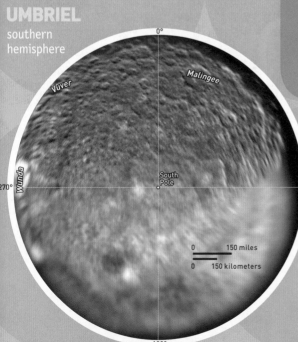

Vuver
Malingee
Wunda
0°
270°
South Pole
90°
180°
0   150 miles
0   150 kilometers

TITANIA
southern hemisphere

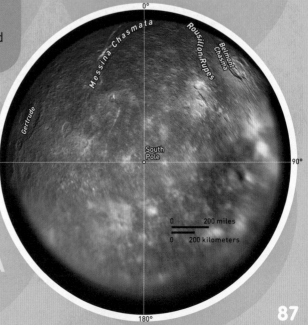

Messina Chasmata
Rousillon Rupes
Belmont Chasma
Gertrude
0°
270°
South Pole
90°
180°
0   200 miles
0   200 kilometers

87

DISTANT NEPTUNE

The "final" PLANET

NEPTUNE DATA

Orbital period: 163.7 Earth years
Rotational period: 16.1 Earth hours
Diameter: 30,775 miles (49,528 km)
Mass: 17.1 Earth's
Density (water=1): 1.6
Gravity: 1.12 Earth's
Average distance from sun:
    2,793 million miles (4,495 million km)
Surface temperature: −353°F (−214°C)
Moons: 14

Neptune

Earth

Deep, blue, cold Neptune. This gas giant is the outermost of all known planets in our solar system. Neptune is as far from Uranus as Saturn is from the sun. Its orbit is so tremendously large that one of its years lasts two human lifetimes. Often known as Uranus's twin, Neptune has a similar size, color, and composition. But it has unique qualities, along with its rings and 14 moons. It's worth going the distance to explore Neptune.

5 COOL FACTS TO RECORD

1 BRING OUT THE BANDS

Neptune's blue makes it seem tranquil, but scientific imaging brings out another story. Sunlight at distant Neptune is weak, but it still grows a little stronger in its springtime, and this is enough to cause seasonal changes. This sequence of images shows the atmosphere getting brighter and cloud belts increasing in width. With a 164-Earth-year orbit, Neptune's spring lasts 40 Earth years.

2 BIG MOON, NEPTUNE!
Spouting forth

Voyager 2's journey past Neptune's largest moon, Triton, caught views of geysers as they spouted a likely mixture of nitrogen, methane, and dust. Erupting as high into the air as five miles (8 km), gas carrying dust hits the cold, freezes, and falls back to Triton's surface as snow. The snow turns rosy when exposed to cosmic rays.

3 MAGNETIC POLES APART

Compared to Earth's magnetic field, Neptune's is "flipped." An ordinary compass would point you generally southward—but not straight south. That's because Neptune's magnetic poles are about halfway to its equator and the magnetic field's center is more than halfway out from the planet's center.

SPACE TRAVEL ATTRACTIONS

GRAB A TELESCOPE!

Neptune is large enough to fit almost 60 Earths inside, but it is too far away for the unaided human eye to see. You'll need a medium-size backyard telescope to see it.

READ ITS TRUE COLORS

Neptune's unique, rich blue—a different shade than Uranus's blue-green—suggests methane and some other substance in its atmosphere.

ZOOM ON SOME MOONS

Do you have an Earth year to spare? Spend most of it—360 Earth days—riding around Neptune just once on its far-out moon, Nereid. Next, hop on box-shaped Proteus for a few, much faster trips around the planet. It takes only 27 hours for Proteus to complete one orbit of Neptune.

4 ANYTHING RING FAMILIAR?

While Voyager 2 confirmed that Neptune, like the other planetary giants, has rings, these six structures have some unique traits. They seem unusually high in dust particles. In addition, each ring varies in thickness, with thicker areas showing as bright arcs that form and then thin out over time.

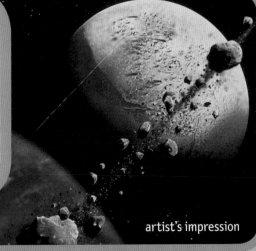

artist's impression

An artist's impression of Neptune—with three of its six rings visible—as seen from the frozen surface of Triton. Distant geysers rupture the surface.

DID YOU KNOW?

Galileo Galilei saw Neptune in the early 1660s but mistook it for a star. Neptune was discovered as a planet in 1846. Its discovery was based on its gravitational pull on Uranus, influencing that planet's orbit.

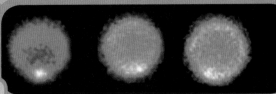

5 KEEPING AN IR OUT

Neptune's extreme weather shifts faster than that of any other gas giant in the solar system. Maps of invisible infrared (IR) energy at its south pole taken at one-month intervals reveal different intensities, showing changes in Neptune's furiously windy upper atmosphere.

A DEEP-BLUE PLANET

An atmosphere of wild STORMS

Neptune as seen by
Voyager 2 in 1998

T he rich, comforting blue of Neptune's atmosphere
may make this planet seem exotic, even inviting.
But behind that tranquil face is a world that would
be difficult to cope with. Frigid temperatures, faint
sunlight, and the solar system's highest global
average wind speed give this planet an extreme environment—
and make it a challenge to explore. Then there's the fascination
of both a natural satellite—the moon Triton—and atmospheric
winds that whirl "backward" to draw you in again.

North Pole

Winds

Bands

Great Dark Spot

EQUATOR

South Pole

0 _____ 4000 miles
0 _____ 4000 kilometers

atmosphere

liquid mantle

core

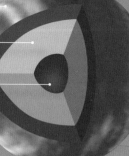

5 COOL FACTS TO RECORD

1. HIGH RISE

Voyager 2's 1989 visit revealed clouds in
Neptune's upper atmosphere that can rise
31 miles (50 km) above their base level. Their
shadows on the layer of clouds below were the
first such shadows seen on another planet. The
clouds are pulled into long, east–west bands.

2. NEPTUNE ANATOMY

Like Uranus, Neptune's gaseous atmosphere contains some
methane and much hydrogen and helium. Below this atmosphere,
these gases liquefy under tremendous pressure from above and
mix with liquid ammonia and water, forming the mantle. (There
is no definite surface layer, or crust.) At the center of it all is,
apparently, an Earth-size, rocky—and dense—core.

DARK, SUNNY DAYS

Even without clouds, anyone who could hypothetically spend time on Neptune would find it dim compared to Earth. This outlying planet is so far from the sun that it only receives 1/900 of the amount of sunshine that bathes Earth. That's about as bright as an overcast day on Earth.

TRITON

top part of the moon has not been mapped

North Pole

MONAD REGIO

0 200 miles

0 200 kilometers

SLIDREGIO

BUBEMBE SULCI

BUBEMBE REGIO

UHLANGA

REGIO

EQUATOR

South Pole

On moon maps, features are often given Latin names. *Regio* is large landmass, and *sulci* are grooves and ridges.

DIGITAL TRAVELER!

Watch a video of two moons orbiting the planet by going to the NASA website and searching for "Neptune dancing with its moons."

GONE WITH THE WIND

Fierce storms on Neptune show up as spots in the atmosphere. Compared to Jupiter's Great Red Spot, or even Saturn's storms, Neptune's storms fade faster. For example, this Great Dark Spot dominated Voyager 2's 1989 picture, but in 1994 scientists using the Hubble Space Telescope confirmed that it was gone.

TRITON'S REVERSE ORBIT

Triton is the only large moon in the solar system to orbit in the direction opposite its planet's rotation. Triton is Neptune's largest natural satellite. Its history may resemble Pluto's. Triton may have been pulled by Neptune's gravity from the Kuiper belt, a way-out part of the solar system (see pages 92–93).

SPACE TRAVEL ATTRACTIONS

GO WINDSURFING—BACKWARD

Let Neptune's winds push you along. You might travel roughly half the width of the United States —about 1,200 miles (1,900 km)—in an hour. Whipping from the east, these currents would take you in a direction opposite most other planets' winds.

SEE TRITON (BEFORE IT GOES)

See Triton's frozen methane and nitrogen ice caps. Watch for spouting geysers, and be sure to catch Neptune rising in Triton's west and setting in the east. See it all now because, in the distant future, Triton may collide with Neptune's cloud tops or perhaps be pulled apart by its strong gravity when it wanders too close.

A LONG, NOT-SO-HOT SUMMER

Neptune's temperature averages about –392°F (–236°C). Yet scientists found that as Neptune's nearly 41-Earth-year-long southern summer slipped toward its end, an area near the south pole did warm significantly. But forget the flip-flops—this "hot" spot was –160°F (–107°C).

91

KUIPER BELT

Rock, ice, and dwarf PLANETS

an artist's conce[pt]
of the spacecraf[t]
New Horizons
nearing the Kuip[er]
belt object, Plut[o]

Ancient skywatchers may not have known everything about the planets, sun, and our moon, but they knew that these objects exist. Thousands of years later, astronomers took some creative leaps. They imagined vast, unseen sections of our solar system, with real, solid objects in them. The Kuiper (KY-per) belt is the nearest of these zones. Just beyond Neptune's orbit, it is a doughnut-shaped disk, 2.32 billion miles (3.73 billion km) wide. Some of our solar system's earliest-formed fragments, along with dwarf planets and moons, have been discovered there, whirling in orbits that take hundreds of years to complete.

5 COOL FACTS TO RECORD

SPACE TRAVEL ATTRACTIONS

➥ KUIPER BELT OBJECTS (KBOs)
Next time you have trouble falling asleep, try counting KBOs. You can expect to tally hundreds of thousands that are each at least as long as Rhode Island, U.S.A.

➥ BRING A FLASHLIGHT
The Kuiper belt is from 30 to 55 times as far from the sun as the Earth is. The closer KBOs might receive just enough sunlight for you to manage to read a book. But bring a flashlight for the more distant regions.

➥ HANG OUT WITH DWARFS
The Kuiper belt is a good place to find dwarf planets, with four of the first five found in this zone: Pluto, Eris, Haumea, and Makemake. (Ceres is in the asteroid belt.) Dozens more Kuiper belt dwarf planets are likely to exist.

1 MORE TO EXPLORE?

In 2006, the New Horizons spacecraft launched toward Pluto. Scientists hoped that while the craft made its way to the Kuiper belt, they would discover other objects close enough to explore after Pluto. In 2014, they found the first possible "nearby" targets—like this one shown in an artist's concept—about 620 million miles (1 billion km) past Pluto.

DID YOU KNOW?

Astronomer Gerard P. Kuiper developed the idea of the Kuiper belt. He noted that comets with orbits that take about 200 years or less should have evaporated long ago, given so much time near the sun. He proposed that icy, comet-like objects were in the solar system beyond Neptune's orbit, and that they become comets when their orbits change.

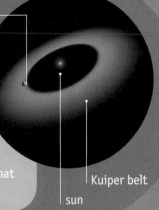

orbit of Neptune

Kuiper belt

sun

3 KUIPER COMET CONNECTION
A tale of tails

An estimated one trillion comets come from the Kuiper belt. You might picture a comet with a long tail streaming behind it, but in the Kuiper belt, comets don't have tails. A tail forms only when a comet's orbit brings it close to the sun. Then, gases and water ice usually frozen in the comet heat up, vaporize, and mix with dust from the comet. These vapors stream from the comet body. From Earth they appear as the comet's tail. Returning to the Kuiper belt, the comet freezes solid again and its tail disappears.

2 JUST DROPPED IN

Two moons in the solar system may be former Kuiper belt residents, caught by their planets' gravity as they strayed out of the belt. They are nearby Neptune's Triton and Saturn's Phoebe, whose irregular surface, imaged by the Cassini spacecraft, provides clues to a former identity as a comet.

Collisions between Kuiper belt objects, as pictured here by an artist, can send icy objects toward the sun. We might see these objects as comets.

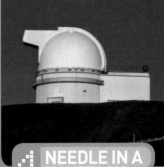

4 NEEDLE IN A HAYSTACK

A powerful telescope at the University of Hawaii observatory helped astronomers David Jewitt and Jane Luu discover the "first" KBO (after Pluto and its moon Charon). About 100 miles (161 km) or so wide, this icy rock that orbits beyond Pluto was officially designated 1992 QB1.

5 THE BIG DEAL?
Ancient chunks

Rocky remnants from the early days of the solar system, KBOs at first resemble asteroids. But unlike asteroids, KBOs have never been warmed by the sun. Scientists think that they are a physical and chemical snapshot of the earliest solids that formed from the disk of gas that became the solar system.

5 COOL FACTS TO RECORD

1 BLUE SKIES ABOVE

Pluto's sky is blue, stretching out in a multilayered haze around the planet. Most likely, the color comes from light bouncing off sootlike particles that form in chemical reactions between nitrogen and methane.

2 PLUTO'S MOONS

Meet Pluto's moons: Charon is largest, Styx seems smallest. Nix and Hydra both tumble unpredictably through space, with no regular day or night. Kerboros—which looks like two stuck-together blobs—is a sign that Pluto and its moons formed from the wreckage of a long-ago collision between two planet-size objects.

PLUTO DATA

Orbital period: 247.9 Earth years
Rotational period: 6.4 Earth days
Diameter: 1,464 miles (2,356 km)
Mass: 0.0025 Earth's
Density (water=1): 2.095
Gravity: 0.071 Earth's
Average distance from sun:
   3,670 million miles (5,906 million km)
Surface temperature: −387°F (−233°C)
Moons: Five

Earth   Pluto

an artist's concept of Pluto and its largest moon, Charon

3 ON THE FACE OF IT
Charon's surface

Although expecting a repetitive landscape of impact craters on the surface of Pluto's largest moon, New Horizons' scientists saw signs of past drama. Charon boasts an impressively long canyon system, signs of landslides, a comparatively new southern surface, and even a mountain in a moat.

DWARF PLUTO

When is a planet not a PLANET?

4 NEW HORIZON

New Horizons' 2015 visit to Pluto was the only close-up exploration of this system. On closest approach it was about 7,767 miles (12,500 km) from Pluto—less than one Earth diameter away. It was 16,777 miles (27,000 km) from Charon. After its long, nine-and-a-half-year journey, its scientific encounter was a brief six months.

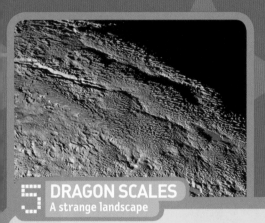

5 DRAGON SCALES
A strange landscape

"Dragon scales"—that's one scientist's description of this scene on Pluto. New Horizons' images show a varied landscape across the entire dwarf planet, including frozen nitrogen glaciers and blocky, water-ice mountains. While there is a "new" surface in the north that is only 10 million years old, southern craters remain unchanged from four billion years ago.

DID YOU KNOW?

According to a teacher, Venetia Burney Phair, Pluto was not named after Disney's star pup. And she should know. As an 11-year-old in 1930, she suggested the then-planet's name. She's on record explaining that she named it after Roman and Greek gods.

In 2006, astronomers reorganized their official lists of objects in space. They did so after discovering several smallish objects that were like planets, but not exactly so. They made a new category for these objects, calling them dwarf planets. To qualify as a dwarf planet, a space object can't be a natural satellite of another: so moons are not dwarf planets. Also, it must be round and share its orbit around the sun with numerous nearby objects, such as fragments of rock. Pluto fits this category—and was taken off the list of planets. Dwarf planet Pluto is the biggest and brightest of this new group.

SPACE TRAVEL ATTRACTIONS

➤ SWING ACROSS NEPTUNE'S PATH
Pluto's orbit crosses Neptune's, but there's no need for a crash helmet. Pluto's orbit is locked in sync with Neptune's and the two never come close to colliding.

➤ SEARCH FOR LIFE
Finding life on Pluto, with its numbing −387°F (−233°C) surface temperature, seems unlikely but there's a surprisingly high amount of methane ice present. Are there methane-expelling microbes living in a warmer sublayer?

➤ FIND THE CENTER
Technically, Pluto's moon Charon does not revolve around the dwarf planet. Their orbits share a common center point in space, as if they ride different spokes on the same wheel—a binary (two-part) dwarf planet system.

RECENT DISCOVERIES

Kuiper belt PLUTOIDS

H aumea, Eris, and Makemake are three smallish objects from the outer solar system. Discovered in the early 2000s, they caused a hullabaloo on Earth that led astronomers to change how they organize and classify space objects. This included making a new category of objects, the dwarf planets (see page 95). Pluto was reclassified as a dwarf planet—along with what was the asteroid Ceres (see pages 66–67). However, some people thought there should be a distinction between Ceres, relatively close to the sun, and the outer dwarf planets. In 2008, astronomers created a subgroup of dwarf planets—the plutoids, named in honor of Pluto. Plutoids are dwarf planets with orbits that take them beyond Neptune's, at least part of the time. Meet Pluto's fellow plutoids—small objects that became a big deal.

an imaginary view of New Horizons spacecraft at Pluto

(see page 95)

(see pages 66–67)

SPACE TRAVEL ATTRACTIONS

GO FOR A SPIN...
...and several other rotations all in one Earth day. You might get dizzy, but you'll flip for fast-turning Haumea. It completes one end-over-end turn every four hours or so.

ENJOY THE HIGH POINT
Eris's orbit is sharply tilted compared to the level of the eight planets. From Eris you can view the planets as if you were on a distant hill, high above them, then as if you were in a valley far below.

WATCH OUT FOR SEDNA
Okay, so Sedna is not a dwarf planet. It's not even from the Kuiper belt. But you can catch this distant, newly discovered object in the Kuiper belt during parts of its orbit.

5 COOL FACTS TO RECORD

1 MAKEMAKE
With a mini moon

Imagine standing on little Makemake (about the same width as Argentina), which was discovered in 2005. At your feet might be rice-size icy pellets—frozen methane. Above would be Makemake's newly discovered 100-mile (161-km) -wide moon—as shown on the right in this artist's

2 EGG-SHAPE
Haumea

Discovered in 2003, does the Pluto-size but elongated

One complete Eris orbit takes a lot of Earth years. One Eris year (557 Earth years) ago today, Christopher Columbus was still a kid.

ERIS MAKES SOME HEAT

Dwarf planet Eris, also discovered in 2005, gets so cold in its far-flung orbit that its entire atmosphere freezes and falls to the planet, coating it like a glaze on a doughnut. It was Eris that sparked astronomers' rethinking of what makes a planet a planet—and led to Pluto's new classification as a dwarf planet.

an artist's depiction of Haumea—one of the oldest known objects in the solar system

M&M COMPOSITION
Hard-shelled

Haumea has a unique, candy-like structure that is unexpected for a KBO (see page 92). Mostly rock, with a glaze of ice over its entire surface, it has been compared to a piece of chocolate with a hard candy shell. But watch out. Although Haumea is usually pretty frozen, unlike those candies, it might melt in your hands.

LITTLE KNOWN MOONS

Not much is known about moons Hi'iaka and Namaka, but bigger Hi'iaka seems to be all ice. This supports the idea that the moons were made of ice knocked off Haumea's icy surface in a collision that also set it spinning head over heels.

DWARF DATA

Distances from the sun of known plutoids:
Pluto: 3,674 million miles (5,913 million km)
Haumea: 4,029 million miles (6,484 million km)
Makemake: 4,254 million miles (6,846 million km)
Eris: 6,289 million miles (10,121 million km)

97

OORT CLOUD

At the edge of our sun's GRAVITY

No one has seen the Oort cloud. No one has touched it. But astronomers have imagined it. It is the assumed last, vast region where the sun's gravitational pull can still hold on to objects, keeping them in orbit. Think of the Oort cloud as the thick glass wall of a snow globe that encompasses everything else in the solar system. Of course it's not glass—just space, through which things move. Here are frozen objects made of the first-formed solids in our solar system. Many have orbits that zoom them toward the sun as comets, taking hundreds, thousands, or more years to shuttle in their loop between the center of the solar system and its farthest reaches.

DID YOU KNOW?

Scientists once thought that the only objects in the Oort cloud were comets. However, some evidence now suggests that there may also be asteroids in the Oort cloud. In fact, there may be as many as eight billion asteroids in the cloud, enough to outnumber the asteroids in the asteroid belt.

5 COOL FACTS TO RECORD

1 OUT IN THE COLD

Four and a half billion years ago, when our solar system was just forming, a giant disk of gas swirled around the new star, our sun. In distant, cold parts of that cloud, bits of materials froze as they were. Over time, much of this matter became the dwarf planets and asteroids. Some remained isolated and unchanged and ultimately swept into what became the Oort cloud.

illustration of sun forming from gas cloud

2 COMET BIRTH

An icy body can stay in the Oort cloud, but if gravity from some passing object tweaks its path, its destiny changes. Now moving sunward, the comet-to-be thaws, waking from its deep freeze. Ice changes to escaping gas. After swinging past the sun, it cools, hibernating as it heads back to the Oort cloud, only to begin another many-Earth-year lap around the sun.

artist's impression of the Oort cloud

3 VIEW FROM OUTER SPACE
A mass of icy bodies

Just as you wouldn't see countries' boundaries if you orbited Earth, no alien observing our solar system would see the Oort cloud as a physical structure. However, paintings help us visualize it. Here, the solar system is represented as if sliced down the middle. Bright blue shows the Oort cloud, where an estimated trillion icy bodies are thought to spend most of their time.

SPACE TRAVEL ATTRACTIONS

➤ STEP IT OUT

In your mind, step out the solar system's milestones on the way to the Oort cloud. Drop a marker for the sun. Take one step to Earth. Continuing, count up to 30 steps—the Kuiper belt's beginning—and 55, its outer edge. Enter the Oort cloud at 5,000. Its outer boundary is at 100,000 steps.

➤ STOP ALONG THE WAY

Seek these points of interest between the Kuiper belt and the Oort cloud: Dwarf planet Eris, whose orbit sometimes takes it outside the Kuiper belt; the Voyager spacecraft; the recently discovered object Sedna; and possible Neptune-size Planet 9 (aka Planet X).

➤ AVOID THE CROWDS

There may be one trillion icy bodies zipping around in the Oort cloud, but as envisioned, it is so huge that these objects are not crowded.

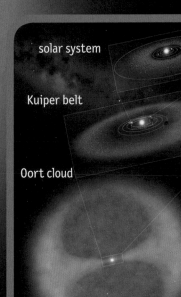

solar system

Kuiper belt

Oort cloud

4 CENTRAL SUN
Holding it together

How small the mighty, central, massive sun must seem from the Oort cloud! However, it is powerful enough to hold the objects in this cloud at the end of its gravity-leash.

5 WHERE IS THE OORT CLOUD?

The Oort cloud is far beyond the planets' orbits. While light from the sun arrives at Neptune in approximately 4 hours, it arrives at the inner Oort cloud in about 693 hours (about 28.9 days). It takes 20 times as much time—578 days (about 1.6 years)—to reach the Oort cloud's outer edge. The Oort cloud is thought to extend in all directions—above, below, and all around the solar system.

CIRCLING COMETS

"Hairy" stars visiting from outer SPACE

comet Lovejoy

Imagine living in a place or distant time where the physical solar system is not well understood. Your community is abuzz about a new, brightening star in the night sky. Light has appeared behind it, growing like long hair. You admire it, maybe fear it. Then it fades from view. This has happened many times across the world and in history. It took many observations, telescopes, and an understanding of orbits to work out the true physical nature of comets. These chunks of icy rock swoop in narrow orbits that bring them close enough to the sun to frizzle their ice and shed their dust.

1 COSMIC COMET CONNECTIONS

Did comets play a starring role in the rise of life on Earth? Over eons, these water-rich bodies may have crashed to Earth, contributing up to one tenth of Earth's current water. Comets also carry substances that support life. For example, recently visited comet 67P/Churyumov-Gerasimenko contains sulphur, alcohols, ammonia, and methane.

2 PHILAE VISIT

On November 12, 2014, the Rosetta mission lander, Philae, touched down on the surface of comet 67P/Churyumov-Gerasimenko. It was the first ever comet landing and long-term visit. Although the mission was not a complete success (see fact 5), the Rosetta spaceship continued to collect data about the comet for almost two more years.

PARTS OF A COMET

tail (dust)

nucleus

to sun

coma

tail (gas)

3 COMET FROM HEAD TO TAIL

The frozen core of a comet is its nucleus. Near the warming sun, its frozen ices vaporize, their gases surrounding the nucleus in a reflective, halo-like atmosphere—the coma. Some escaping gases and loosened dust are also pushed back by the solar wind. This creates the comet's tail (actually two separate tails). Invisible, lightweight hydrogen envelops the coma and tail, and can stretch for millions of miles (km).

a comet's orbit around the sun

sun

comet

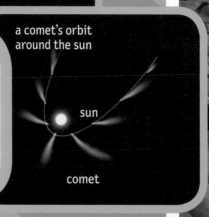

SPACE TRAVEL ATTRACTIONS

❹ RETURNING LIKE CLOCKWORK

Astronomer Edmond Halley suspected that certain "different" comets in history were regular visits of the same one. He correctly predicted a 1758 reappearance. "His" comet returned in 1834, 1910, and 1986. Although it won't return until 2061, bits of its tail remain across Earth's orbit and are visible as parts of the yearly Orionid and Eta Aquarid meteor showers.

➤ DON'T WAIT UP

In 1996 comet Hyakutake, discovered by an amateur astronomer, wowed skywatchers. It displayed an especially long, bright, colorful tail and big coma. Don't wait for it to reappear. It's not due back until the year 31,496.

➤ SOHO CLOSE TO THE SUN

Watch comets swing through the inner solar system or evaporate completely with the Solar and Heliospheric Observatory (SOHO). It was designed for sun-watching, but because it blocks most of the sun's bright glare, SOHO has turned out to be a great comet hunter.

➤ BREAK SPEED RECORDS

Hop on a sungrazer comet, one that gets extremely close to the sun. It zooms fast enough to whip around Earth in one minute.

an artist's impression of Philae landing on a comet

❺ BUMPY LANDING
Philae spacecraft

The Rosetta spaceship image below of comet 67P/Churyumov-Gerasimenko shows its uneven surface. Ice screws, anchoring harpoons, and a down-pushing thruster should have kept the lander Philae on the low-gravity surface. But Philae bounced—about 3,300 feet (1,006 m) high! It then soared, spun, and tumbled above the comet for two hours before finally settling down.

DIGITAL TRAVELER!
Find out what it is like to land on a comet with this simulated animation of Philae's journey from its mother spaceship Rosetta, based on data from the landing: search the Internet for "space in videos 2015 11 reconstructing Philae's flight ESA."

OUR GALAXY AND BEYOND

Getting a sense of PROPORTION

I t may not be obvious from here on Earth, but our solar system is huge. It takes eight minutes for the light of our sun to reach Earth, but 1.6 years to reach the Oort cloud's outer edge. Yet even our giant solar system is a tiny speck compared to the community of stars to which it belongs—our home galaxy, the Milky Way. Much larger still is the entire universe. Exploring our galaxy and the universe is exciting because there is so much to discover. Check out the details as you cross the threshold into the rest of the Milky Way ... and beyond!

AUNT BERTHA'S SPACE TRAVEL TIPS

Start measuring with the light-year—the distance light can travel in one year through total emptiness. At light's speed of 671 million miles an hour (1,080 million km/h), in one year it would go almost six trillion miles (9.7 trillion km).

Take it all in—Earth and the sky by night and day. Except for the Andromeda galaxy (Northern Hemisphere) and the Magellanic Clouds (Southern Hemisphere), what you can see with unaided eyes is all part of the Milky Way.

Travel through time—sort of. Light reaching you from vast distances shows what was happening when it left its source long ago. Just by looking at space, you see what was, not what is.

The universe is constantly changing. This is an artist's impression of two galaxies, each packed with stars, colliding deep in space.

THE MILKY WAY

A swirling cloud of luminous STARS

spiral galaxy
Messier 51

You have probably seen pictures of the Milky Way on T-shirts, in advertisements, or on the Internet. But no one has actually ever seen the Milky Way from the outside. The images—including the one here—are scientists' best maps based on what they see and measure from the inside. Ancient peoples saw our galaxy as many stars and a bright, milky glow splashed across the night sky. Only 100 years or so ago, astronomers recognized that the Milky Way is just one of many galaxies. Like all galaxies, it is a vast population of billions of stars in a gravity-bound huddle, drifting as a group like a floating island in a sea. Let's explore the Milky Way, your home island in space.

SPACE TRAVEL ATTRACTIONS

DRINK IT IN
If at all possible, visit the countryside for a deep, long look at the night sky. It's simple to do, and marvelous beyond words.

KNOW THE "WAY"
Notice a band of light extending across the sky, glowing with a milky light. To ancients, it looked like a path, or "way." Today, "Milky Way" means both this band and our whole galaxy.

A NEW VIEW
Visit the galactic bulge. From inside the bulge, enjoy brilliant starlight in all directions. From Earth, you see the bulge as a bright patch along a band of light crossing the sky, which is the disk seen edge-on.

5 COOL FACTS TO RECORD

1 GIANT SPIRAL
Beaded arms

Seen from above, our galaxy would most likely appear as a spiral with several arms and a tremendously bright, central sphere. Dust, gases, and 200 billion or more luminous stars orbit in an expansive, flattened disk around the center. It takes about 230 million years for our solar system to complete one trip around the center. From edge to edge, the Milky Way is about 100,000 light-years wide (see page 102).

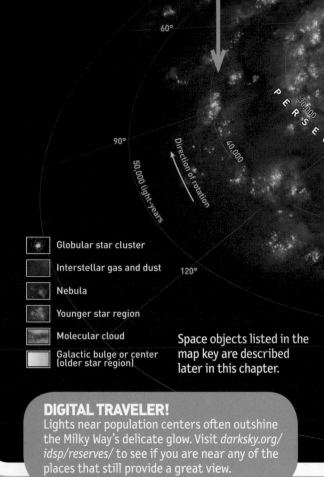

60°

90°

120°

PERSEUS

30,000

40,000

50,000 light-years

Direction of rotation

- ● Globular star cluster
- ■ Interstellar gas and dust
- ■ Nebula
- ■ Younger star region
- ▨ Molecular cloud
- ▢ Galactic bulge or center (older star region)

Space objects listed in the map key are described later in this chapter.

DIGITAL TRAVELER!
Lights near population centers often outshine the Milky Way's delicate glow. Visit *darksky.org/idsp/reserves/* to see if you are near any of the places that still provide a great view.

2 GALACTIC BULGE
A dense star neighborhood

The rounded, central bump of our galaxy is crowded with stars. Imagine that for every star present in one of the arms, there are probably several hundred thousand stars located in the bulge. The collective light from the tens of millions of stars in the bulge is seen from Earth as the brightest glow in the Milky Way, near the constellation Sagittarius.

3 NEBULA
Fuzzy language

Scattered across the Milky Way are features called nebulas. As astronomers began to peer through telescopes, they noticed fuzzy or hazy patches of light. They called them nebulas, based on the Latin word for a cloud, *nebula*. There are different types of nebulas, but in general they are irregularly shaped, massive clouds of mostly hydrogen and helium gas, with some dust. Some nebulas, such as the Orion Nebula, are where stars form.

4 YOUNG STARS
Born from compressed gases

To find young, hot stars, head to the spiral arms of the Milky Way. The stars form from dense, massive clouds of hydrogen with such tightly compressed centers that atoms are forced together. This fusion of atoms releases a tremendous amount of energy—the star's light, heat, and motion.

artist's impression

330°
300°
270°
240°
0°

FAR 3 KPC ARM
NEAR 3 KPC ARM
NORMA ARM
SCUTUM-CENTAURUS ARM
SAGITTARIUS ARM
10,000
20,000
SAGITTARIUS ARM
OUR SOLAR SYSTEM
ORION SPUR
3,000
6,000 light-years
210°
180°
150°
ARM
OUTER ARM

a map of the Milky Way, with our solar system some 26,000 light years from the center

5 DARK NEBULAS
Molecular clouds

Stars form deep within dark molecular clouds called dark nebulas. Despite the starlight within, they seem dark to us because dust within molecular clouds blocks visible light. However, microwave and infrared light pass through, so scientists can detect these waves and investigate these clouds. You can glimpse dark nebulas as the vast dark patches in the Milky Way.

EXOPLANETS

Other stars with orbiting PLANETS

Hello? Is there anybody out there? Is Earth one of a kind or one of a zillion or more similar planets? What clues can we gather about how our planet and solar system developed by peering at other systems? Curiosity drives our search for exoplanets, which are planets orbiting stars other than our sun. But there are so many stars, each distant and huge in comparison to the planets we know. How could we possibly hope to find a planet in a star's glare? The answer is with a wobble. A slight wobble of a star led to the first confirmed exoplanet discovery, in 1992. Today we count exoplanets by the thousands!

SPACE TRAVEL ATTRACTIONS

WATCH THE WOBBLE
How do you pinpoint an exoplanet to visit? Seek signs of a gravitational tug between a star and a planet. The star wobbles as it moves slightly toward the orbiting planet. Fine measurements reveal the wobble and clue you in to the planet's size, orbit, and mass.

(DON'T) SEE THE LIGHT
As any planet orbits its star, it regularly comes between Earth and its sun, blotting out a small disk of light. The light reaching us will dip just a bit and is sometimes a detectable clue to a planet's presence.

VISIT HISTORIC SITES
The first three exoplanets discovered (in 1992) orbit a pulsar (see page 123). Exoplanet 51 Pegasi b, discovered in 1995, was the first to be found orbiting a regular star (51 Pegasi). This planet is half Jupiter's mass and takes just four Earth days to complete its year.

5 COOL FACTS TO RECORD

1 SEEKING PLANETS
Twelve years after confirming the first exoplanets, astronomers finally found an Earth-size planet in a star's habitable zone (see fact 5). Kepler-186f is dimly lit as it orbits a star about half the size of Earth's sun.

2 CLOSER TO HOME
In 2015, a near-Earth-size planet was confirmed orbiting a sun-like star's habitable zone. This exoplanet was named Kepler-452b. Finds of planets similar to Earth continue to pile up. Discovering a true twin is probably a matter of time, technology, and patience.

artist's concept of Kepler-452b

2 AU (299,200,000 km)
1 AU (149,600,000 km)
KEPLER 22
KEPLER 22b
A p p r o x i m a t e   H a b i t a b l e   Z o n e

3 HABITABLE ZONE

Also known as the Goldilocks Zone, where everything is just right, the habitable zone is the belt of space around a star where terrestrial planets could form, hold liquid water, and support life. However, ideas about this zone may change, given new findings. For example, outside our solar system's habitable zone, oceans (and potentially life) may exist beneath some moons' ice sheets.

NAMING EXOPLANETS

In general, an exoplanet is named after the star it orbits or the scientific instrument or space mission that led to its discovery. A lower case letter tells the order in which the planets around the star were discovered. The host star is always labeled "a." For example, Kepler-186f was the fifth exoplanet discovered around the 186th star that was found to have planets orbiting it in the Kepler space survey.

an artist's depiction of a star (far left) with several planets, one covered in ice (seen close up spanning the top of the image) and one with a moon and rings (below)

4 FIRST LOOK

Fine measurements are the key to discovering exoplanets. Most have not been imaged. In 2004, a very powerful telescope captured one of the first images of an exoplanet (the red spot in this colorized view). It orbits a star-like brown dwarf (see pages 114–115), 171 light-years from Earth. Its name is 2MASS J12073346-3932539 b, but astronomers also call it 2M1207b for short.

5 MEET THE HUNTER

The Kepler spacecraft, launched in 2009, is a major contributor to finding exoplanets. In its first seven years of operation, it has found more than 2,300 confirmed and almost 5,000 possible exoplanets.

ALIEN WORLDS

Exoplanets and the possibility of LIFE-FORMS

A lien life exists—at least in our minds! Currently, life anywhere except Earth is the stuff of science fiction. Writers, moviemakers, computer game creators, and visual artists may use scientific ideas as a starting point for what aliens might look like, but they let their imaginations run wild. Their ideas range from insect-like creatures on an infrared planet to pseudosharks in an underwater world. Exobiologists, astrobiologists, and many others all explore similar questions when it comes to extraterrestrial life. What other possibilities for life are out there? How might alien life compare to what we know?

an imaginary exoplanet alien

DID YOU KNOW?

As of May 2016, the total number of possible alien worlds were 3,413 confirmed exoplanets, 4,696 possible exoplanets identified, and 533 multiplanet star systems. (The figures include the exoplanets found specifically by the Kepler spacecraft—see page 107.)

1. LOW GRAVITY WORLDS

It is estimated that exoplanet Kepler-11f possesses just less than one-third of Earth's gravity. On a similar exoplanet, trees and animals might grow tall and spindly because there is less force to literally weigh them down. Here, a 10-foot (3-m)-tall, imaginary low-gravity exoplanet creature *Antilla* towers above its fungus-like food source.

2. INFRARED WORLD

Exoplanet Kepler-186f orbits a dwarf star (see page 114). Much of the radiation from a dwarf star is infrared light, which humans cannot see. Could life exist on such a planet? Even on Earth a few plants and bacteria in murky waters trap and use infrared light energy in photosynthesis. Somewhere on an exoplanet like Kepler-186f, perhaps there are insect-like life-forms that feed on infrared-dependent plants.

WATERY WORLD

A mostly or even all-ocean world seems likely to host diverse life-forms, with food chains and food webs. Scientists think life on Earth probably first took hold in the ocean. The distant exoplanet HAT-P-11b shows signs of water vapor in its air. Might it possibly be a watery world ... with giant sharks that hunt spiny fish?

DYING WORLD

Exoplanet HD 88512b may once have been in its star's habitable zone. As a planet's star changes, it's likely the planet's environment will alter dramatically. Perhaps as a star dies (see pages 110–111), many life-forms, such as trees and other terrestrial plants, will begin to disappear from the landscape, leaving animals such as these imaginary exoplanet creatures to forage in wetland areas.

EXTREME CONDITIONS

In Earth's oceans, deep beneath the surface, high-pressure and high-temperature zones were once thought impossible as places to find life—until scientists found bacteria, worms, and limpets around thermal vents. On a harsh world like exoplanet Kepler-69c, perhaps imaginary creatures like this 20-ton (18-t) tennet could exist, lumbering on many legs for support against the dense atmosphere.

DIGITAL TRAVELER!
Get the scoop on the search for alien life in our solar system and beyond. Watch a NOVA episode online. Search for "NOVA Finding Life Beyond Earth PBS." If you want to explore the latest on exoplanet discovery, search for and visit the NASA Exoplanet Archive.

STARS

Birth, life, and death of STARS

Galaxies are full of stars, each formed from an enormous cloud of dust and gas, composed mostly of hydrogen. The cloud is known as a nebula. Gravity pulls parts of the cloud together, and little by little the gases form a central mass. A sphere forms. Heavy outer layers crush inward and press down on the center. This compresses the mass until its hydrogen atoms can no longer remain separate. They squish together, or fuse, transforming into helium. This fusion reaction comes with an enormous release of energy in different forms—heat, the zooming motion of tiny particles, and what we see as starlight. This is the birth of the star. After this birth, the star will continue to fuse atoms in its core and release energy until no more fusible atoms are left. The star then dies.

SPACE TRAVEL ATTRACTIONS

CONSIDER REINCARNATION
Stars are born in clouds of gas (upper left in the main illustration). They end by shedding clouds of gas, some of which may be reincarnated as new stars.

VISIT A DUMBBELL AND A RING
Fly by the Dumbbell Nebula, found in the constellation Vulpecula (the Little Fox), and the Ring Nebula, in Lyra (the Lyre). Take a look. Do they remind you of fading planets or Uranus? Early observers thought so. That's why these cloudy features were dubbed planetary nebulas.

WATCH YOUR WEIGHT
The small, dense cores of old stars gravitationally pull very hard on anything near them. Your weight would be dramatically different on different stars: 100,000 times more on a white dwarf (see fact 3) and 200 billion times more on a neutron star (fact 5) than it is on Earth.

5 COOL FACTS TO RECORD

1 SMALL STARS
Forming red giants

Stars like our sun burn steadily for billions of years before the core runs out of hydrogen. Some hydrogen is in the outer layers and begins fusing after the core runs out, but with less intensity. The heating outer layers puff out and the star grows to several times its original size. The lower-energy giant glows red, like embers in a dying fire. It's now a red giant. (Follow the yellow arrows on illustration.)

2 MASSIVE STARS
Fast, furious, and blue

With at least five times the mass of our sun, high-mass stars have a lot of fuel. It fuses quickly in the intense pressure cookers of their cores. These big stars burn hot and bright with a bluish tinge. Compared to less massive stars, these blue giants don't last long—maybe one million years or so. (Follow the green arrows for this story.)

THE STORY OF STAR

route of low- and medium-mass stars like the sun

nebula

route of massive stars

blue giant

TIME TRAVELER!
Grab a night-sky guide, head to an area with little artificial light, and try spotting nebulas and nebula-like features, all of which are somewhat cloudy looking. In the Northern Hemisphere, see the Lagoon Nebula, the Great Rift, and the Orion Nebula. In the Southern Hemisphere, seek out the Large and Small Magellanic Clouds and the Coalsack and Carina Nebulas.

When it comes to stars, the amount of matter matters—a lot. The original mass of the star dictates its future. This illustration shows a simplified story of the birth, life, and death of stars. There are two sequences to follow, as indicated by the yellow (top) and green (bottom) arrows.

3 SMALL, DIM, DENSE
White dwarf

A red giant ends with a brief sputter and sheds its outer gases. The core is now a small, dim, and dense white dwarf star, and the departing, glowing gas cloud is a so-called planetary nebula. After the cloud drifts away, the white dwarf slowly cools and dies.

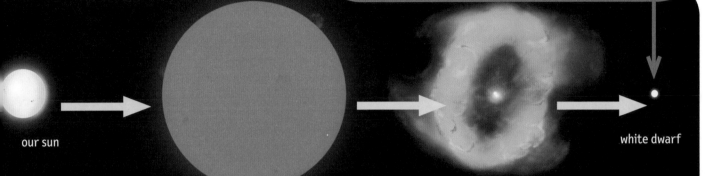

our sun

red giant

planetary nebula

white dwarf

OUR GALAXY AND BEYOND

neutron star

black hole ... or

red supergiant

supernova

4 RED SUPERGIANTS
Bigger and redder

The red supergiant phase is a high-mass star's version of a red giant. The core runs out of hydrogen and it begins to collapse. This brings outer layers closer together. The hydrogen in them compacts enough to fuse. With these outer layers free to expand and continued heating from the fusion, the already giant star becomes a supergiant but with lower temperatures. It now glows red.

5 TWO POSSIBILITIES
Neutron star or black hole

The end phase of a massive star begins with one of the universe's most enormous explosions—a supernova. Outer layers blast away from the core. What's left behind? Perhaps a small core, about 10 miles (16.1 km) wide, jam-packed with the mass of multiple suns. This is an energy-emitting neutron star. Or, if the core is somewhat denser, it becomes a black hole—where gravity pulls so strongly that not even light can travel away from it.

111

CYGNUS
HERCULES
Vega
α
β
γ
M57
[Ring Nebula]
M56
LYRA

1 A MOMENT OF REFLECTION

A nebula, energized from the blast of a dying star, might glow with its own light. But a brand-new star, V380 Orionis, burning hot and bright, illuminates this reflected nebula, named NGC 1999.

2 RING NEBULA
M57 in Lyra

The famous Ring Nebula, visible with telescopes, is made of a dying star and glowing rings of the gas that it has shed. It lies in the constellation Lyra.

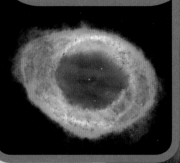

3 SEEING IN THE DARK
Orion's Horsehead Nebula

This part of the Horsehead Nebula, usually shadowy and dark because its dust absorbs visible light, reveals a delicate structure thanks to infrared imaging that pierces the dust. New stars shine at the edges, still embedded in the gas cloud from which they formed.

DID YOU KNOW?

In Australian Aboriginal culture, dark nebulas are important in astrological folklore. For example, dark patches in the Milky Way form the Emu in the Sky. In the same culture, stars in the constellation Orion are said to trace the shape of a canoe with three fishermen sitting side by side and a fishing line trailing behind.

central bulge

NEBULAS
Spectacular clouds of atoms and DUST

planetary nebula NGC 7662

4 STELLAR NURSERY
Carina Nebula

Astronomers can tell that baby stars are just coming into their own even though they are unseen deep within this three-light-year-tall "mountain" of gas and dust. In this colorized image, astronomers recognize the glowing hot, charged streamers of gas shooting off the top of the "peak" as a sign of star birth.

DIGITAL TRAVELER!

Follow the lead of thousands of amateur astronomers by exploring the Messier catalog at *messier.seds.org/Messier.html*. Beginning in 1760, comet hunter Charles Messier made this list of fuzzy patches that seemed like comets but were in fact nebulas, galaxies, and star clusters (see pages 124–125).

5 OUT OF THIS GALAXY
Historic spiral nebula

Early telescopic photographs revealed spiral-shaped fuzzy patches—the "spiral nebulas" that puzzled astronomers. Today seen in highly detailed images, Andromeda was the first mysterious spiral to be understood as a galaxy beyond the Milky Way. Here, part of its central bulge (left) and spiral arms can be seen.

spiral arms

P eering through early telescopes, astronomers saw circular and pinpoint space objects, as well as cloudlike wisps. They concluded that the circular objects were spheres (planets), the pinpoints were stars, and any fixed, cloudlike objects were nebulas. Now we know that a few nebulas turned out to be whole galaxies; some are clusters of stars; and still others are single stars encircled by rings of gas. So what exactly is a nebula? It's officially considered a cloud of stellar gas, sometimes mixed with dust. Some nebulas form with the birth of a star, others with the death of a star (see pages 110–111). They might glow with their own light, reflect starlight, or absorb it. One thing they all have in common? They are stunning to look at.

SPACE TRAVEL ATTRACTIONS

GIVE IT A SIDELONG GLANCE
To see a faint nebula, direct your glance slightly away from it. This aligns the most light-sensitive parts of your eyes with the nebula. Try this strategy to view the Orion Nebula in the constellation Orion (the Hunter).

AS BLACK AS COAL
Peer into the deep of the Coalsack Nebula of the Southern Hemisphere, featuring dark, stellar dust. The dust is so dense that it hides the light of stars behind it, blacking them out from our view.

MULTIPLE STARS
Swing your sight to the Swan, or Omega, Nebula in the constellation Sagittarius. It contains enough hydrogen to make hundreds of stars like our sun.

113

5 COOL FACTS TO RECORD

1 ORION NEBULA
First lights

Orion—the imaginary figure of a hunter—commands the northern winter sky. The constellation's right armpit boasts impressive, dying, red supergiant Betelgeuse (sounds like "beetle juice"). Yet, tucked under Orion's sword is the faintly glowing Orion Nebula, feverish with new star birth. Dim to the unaided eye, the nebula's brilliant energy shines in telescopic views.

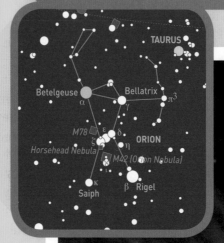

2 STAR FIELD

The total number of stars in the night sky that are visible with the naked eye is about 9,000. At the North Pole or South Pole, you may be able to see about 4,500 of these stars. At other locations, under the darkest sky, you can probably see no more than about 3,500. This Hubble Space Telescope (HST) image is a reminder that the Milky Way galaxy is loaded with many more stars—100 billion or more.

SPACE TRAVEL ATTRACTIONS

⬩ GET SIRIUS

From Earth we can only see a star's apparent brightness—how bright it *seems* rather than how bright it is. For example, Sirius appears as the brightest star in our sky, but Bellatrix, found northwest of Sirius, actually burns about 250 times more brightly.

⬩ LEARN YOUR OBAFGKM's

In the early 1900s, astronomers categorized stars based on their color. Each category received a letter. Later, the list was ordered from the hottest to the coolest star types: O, B, A, F, G, K, M.

⬩ COMPARE COLORS

Grab a star guide. Do you notice the differences in these stars' colors? The white-blue of Spica, the blue of Sirius, the yellow of Procyon and Polaris, and the red of Arcturus and Aldebaran. (It's not easy.)

3 BROWN DWARFS

Between a full-fledged star and a less massive gas giant planet are spheres of gas too small to ignite and blaze steadily but heavy enough to spark and fizzle. These brown dwarfs are 13 to 75 times Jupiter's mass and they emit infrared rays. They probably have atmospheres and storms, too.

artist's concept of a brown dwarf

ALL-STARS

Varied sizes and COLORS

OUR GALAXY AND BEYOND

4 WOLF-RAYET NEBULA

Wolf-Rayet (WR) stars are a late stage of some massive stars. A WR star packs a punch. Temperatures reach at least 36,000°F (19,982°C), and it shines one million times as brightly as our sun. With this much energy, it ejects a lot of matter, which then forms a bubble-like nebula around the star.

If you stargaze for a while, you may notice that, like gemstones in a treasure chest, star sizes and colors vary. Some differences have to do with circumstances outside the stars. For example, their distances from Earth vary, and a distant star is likely to look dimmer than it would from close-up. There are also built-in differences between the stars. One of these is how much matter was in a star when it first formed (its mass). And its mass relates to its other features. It affects the pressure in the core of the star, and that influences how fast the star consumes its fuel and how hot it is. Our sun is yellow in color: Its temperature is about 10,000°F (5538°C). Hotter stars are white or bluish-white (up to 100,000°F [55,388°C]). Cooler stars are orange, red, or dark brown in color, with temperatures down to 6000°F (3316°C).

5 COLORFUL CONCLUSIONS

In general, a star's color reveals its temperature. That's because gases at different temperatures glow with specific colors. Temperature, combined with the mass of a star, can tell astronomers the star's actual brightness (luminosity), how long it will shine, and how it will die.

O star (blue)

B star (blue-white)

A star (white)

F star (yellow-white)

G star—our sun (yellow)

red giant star

K star (orange)

M star (red)

white dwarf

In this diagram, the hottest star is shown top left, the coolest bottom right. A white dwarf starts very hot but cools as the star dies (see page 111). A red giant is very cool.

VARIABLE STARS

When stars FLICKER

giant star
Eta Carinae

DID YOU KNOW?

In 1923, Edwin Hubble discovered a Cepheid variable star in a faint nebula. Using this star to measure the nebula's distance from Earth, he showed that it was so far that it must be well outside the Milky Way and a galaxy in its own right.

5 COOL FACTS TO RECORD

Earth's atmosphere can make stars seem to twinkle, or shimmer, because of currents and other changes in the air between us and the stars. Setting aside that twinkle, there are more than 150,000 stars whose brightness appears to change in intensity over time—days, weeks, months, or more. These are the variable stars. The brightness of a variable star increases, fades, then increases again in cycles. While the stars are too far away for astronomers to visit them, with observations and reasoning, they have worked out some of the causes of the variability. Each explanation highlights the ways stars in the universe are born, live, and die.

1 ERUPTIVE VARIABLES

With irregular timing, these rare supergiants suddenly fade to one-thousandth their usual brightness then regain their original brilliance over a period of months. The Dust Puff Theory explains this behavior. Ferocious surface explosions thrust material outward. It eventually cools and solidifies, forming a huge dust cloud. Hidden behind the cloud, the star seems to dim, then brighten slowly as dust drifts away, as in this illustration.

SPACE TRAVEL ATTRACTIONS

A DEMON'S EYE
Head to Perseus, a constellation named after the mythological slayer of snake-haired Medusa. The star named Algol, or "blinking demon," represents one of Medusa's eyes. It brightens, dims, and brightens again, every 2.87 days.

STAR IN ANOTHER MONSTER
Mira is a variable red giant star in the constellation Cetus (the Sea Monster). Over 11-month cycles, Mira expands, brightens, then contracts and dims to invisibility—and brightens again.

SUPER STARGAZER STATUS
Feel like challenging yourself to observe and document variable stars? Try to match the likes of Leslie C. Peltier, whose 132,000 observations of variable stars helped advance our knowledge of these space objects.

116

2 CEPHEIDS
RS Puppis

Cepheid variable stars are handy to astronomers. The timing of a Cepheid's light cycle is locked into how intensely the star actually burns. Comparing how bright it *looks* to how bright it *should be*, astronomers can figure out its distance from Earth—6,500 light-years for RS Puppis, a star in the southern constellation Puppis, which cycles every six weeks.

3 NO TIME TO MELLOW OUT

T Tauri stars—like the heavily spotted star in this illustration—may show us how our sun behaved very early on. Young stars with about the same mass as our sun take time to settle into stardom. While immature, they burst into bright activity, then calm down and dim, then flare again with irregular timing and changes in brightness.

5 BINARY STARS

Sometimes, what looks like one star is actually two rotating around each other. As one orbits the other, it might come between Earth and its companion. This can block the companion's light and make the system dim until the eclipse ends.

concept illustration

4 ERUPTING STARS
Eta Carinae

Eta Carinae is a system of two giant stars. Every 5.5 years, the stars get extremely close to one another, their solar winds interact—as in this artist's impression—and their light signals change dramatically.

A SLOW, RED DEATH

When stars run out of FUEL

S tars have lots of fusion going on—the crushing together of atomic centers—creating a new type of atom. For example, during most of a star's life, hydrogen in the core fuses to helium. Running out of hydrogen causes a collapse, temporarily boosting the core pressure so that helium atoms are fused—forming carbon atoms. When helium runs out, the fusion cycle starts again. Eventually, iron atoms are formed. However, with each round, it takes more pressure and higher temperatures to join the products of the previous fusion into atoms of another element. With less excess energy, the hot star material cools just a bit. It glows red, like the red coals in a dying fire.

IT'S ELEMENTARY

Hydrogen, helium, and carbon are all chemical elements and are among the lightest of all naturally occurring elements in the universe. Uranium is the heaviest common element.

LEAVE A MESSAGE IN STAR DUST

Pick up a pencil with graphite lead and write a message. Graphite is a type of carbon. All carbon was made in a star somewhere, sometime in the universe. Your message is written in star dust!

BEWARE OF IMPOSTERS

The most common star type is red—not a red giant or supergiant but a red dwarf. Red dwarfs start out as small, slow-burning, mellow, red stars. As you cruise the galaxy, check out red dwarfs Proxima Centauri and Barnard's star, fewer than six light-years from Earth.

a vision of our sun becoming a red giant

COOL FACTS TO RECORD

1. SUN-SIZE STARS

How big will our sun become as a red giant in five billion years? Big enough to stretch out to just beyond Earth's current orbit. That means it will grow from its current diameter—864,337 miles (1,391,016 km)—to a new, estimated diameter of about 209 million miles (336 million km).

2. SUPERGIANT FUSION CYCLES

The greater a star's mass, the more fusion cycles it will have. With each cycle, lots of energy is released, making the star expand like a balloon being inflated. However, the fusion of iron atoms saps the star of energy. Fusion stops. The star dies. Heavier elements such as silver, gold, and copper are made not in stars but in high-pressure, superhot supernovas. In this artwork, the nuclei of two atoms (left) fuse (to form the central mass) and then create a new nucleus (top right), a neutron (bottom right), and lots of energy.

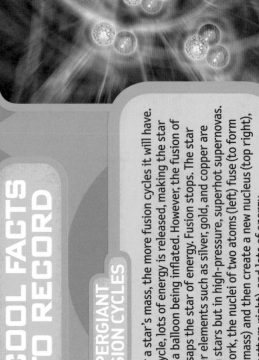

Fusion has been going on in our sun for about 4.5 billion years. As a medium-mass star, its total time fusing hydrogen will be about 10 billion years. It will last as a red giant for about 1 billion additional years. High-mass stars churn through their fuel at much higher rates. Their expected lifetimes last an estimated tens of millions of years. The image of this red supergiant is blurred by Earth's atmosphere.

SUPERGIANTS ARE GIANT
A supernova in the making

The star Betelgeuse in the constellation Orion (the Hunter) is the tenth brightest star in the night sky. (Nearby Rigel, a blue-white star, is seventh.) If this red supergiant replaced our sun in the solar system, it would reach out past the asteroid belt, almost to Jupiter. That's 1,000 times as big as our sun is now.

Massive red giant Betelgeuse engulfs a small moon in this imagined scene.

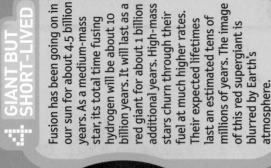

TAURUS

π³

ORION

Bellatrix

γ

λ

δ

M78

ζ

η

M42 (Orion Nebula)

β Rigel

κ

Horsehead Nebula

Saiph

Betelgeuse

α

DIMMER BUT BRIGHT

Which is brighter—a red giant or the small star from which it formed (see pages 110–111)? Both! How can this be? Comparing small, same-size patches on both stars, you'll find the red giant's patch emits about 80 percent less light: It is dimmer. However, with a bigger size, the red giant has many more patches. It gives off more total light, appearing perhaps 100 times brighter.

DID YOU KNOW?

When the sun becomes a red giant and expands to Earth's orbit, Earthlings may not need to pack up and move. Red giants lose matter over time, and their gravitation decreases. Earth's orbit may grow big enough to escape the advance of the sun.

DIGITAL TRAVELER!
To watch an animation video about how atoms fuse in stars, go to pbslearningmedia.org. Once there, search the site for "resource ess05 elements forged in stars."

OUR GALAXY AND BEYOND

5 COOL FACTS TO RECORD

1 FLASH FINISH

In 2011, astronomers measured a supernova whose flash was 130 million times our sun's brightness. Eventually it grew to be one billion times as bright. At 1.2 billion light-years away, the supernova was too far to see with unaided eyes. This artist's impression shows that any nearby planet would become a dead world.

SPACE TRAVEL ATTRACTIONS

COUNT THE SECONDS
Keep a safe distance as you watch matter surge from a supernova at amazing speeds. Time it: Count one second ... stop! In that second, the star's material travels 18,640 miles (29,998 km)—more than two Earth diameters.

LOOK BUT DON'T BLINK
Between now and 2063, chances are 20 percent that the supernova of a Milky Way star will be visible from Earth to the unaided eye. Keep watch so you don't miss it.

A SPECTACULAR SIGHT
With an X-ray telescope aimed at the constellation Lupus (the Wolf), astronomers can see remnants of a supernova that Earthlings witnessed during daytime in the year 1006. According to descriptions at the time, the supernova changed color and threw out visible sparks.

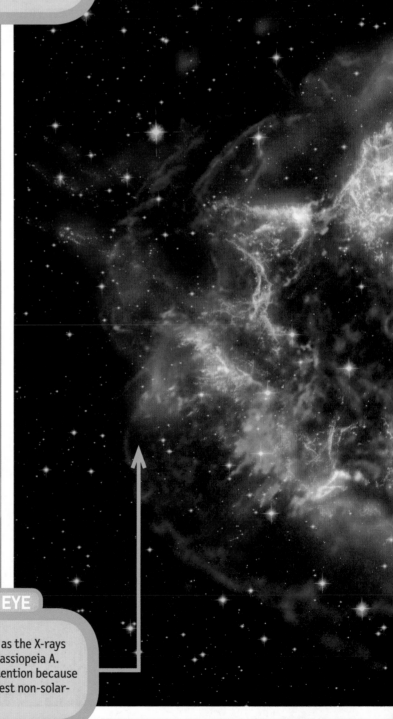

2 BEYOND WHAT MEETS THE EYE
Cassiopeia A's energy

Supernovas give off many types of energy, such as the X-rays that are mapped in this color-coded image of Cassiopeia A. Cassiopeia A originally caught astronomers' attention because of its radio energy. The supernova is the strongest non-solar-system radio energy source in Earth's sky.

SUPER-NOVA!
What a BLAST

3 CASSIOPEIA A
Supernova remnant in X-ray

A star becomes a supernova—then what? Three or four hundred years after its explosive ending, one former star's gases are still advancing outward as an expanding gas bubble. Seen in this colorized X-ray image, the supernova remnant Cassiopeia A measures about 10 light-years across. It lies within the constellation of the same name.

CASSIOPEIA
ε
γ Tsih
M52
δ Caph
Ruchbah β
η
α
Shedar

The last gasp of a massive star—at least eight times as big as our sun—is a giant, flashy supernova that blasts most of the star's matter into space. It begins when fusion in the star stops. Its internal furnace cools. Immediately, the star's cooling core shrinks as gravity crushes it inward. Suddenly, the star's outer layers have no support. They free-fall inward until—wham! They hit the compressed core and ricochet outward. In minutes, the ball of gas grows to several times the star's original size and shines more brightly than ever. Spewing, tumbling matter, searing heat, and blinding light: This is a supernova!

4 LARGE MAGELLANIC CLOUD

A supernova in the nearby Large Magellanic Cloud galaxy caused a stir when it happened in 1987. And it continues to do so today. Using the Hubble Space Telescope, astronomers observe the spectacular after-effects, as in this image of the luminous glow of a ring of gases that once surrounded the star.

5 SUPERNOVAS FOR SCIENCE

Astronomers use some types of supernovas, categorized as Type 1A's, to map space. Like identical light bulbs, they all shine with equal brightness. Using measurements of a Type 1A's brightness, astronomers can calculate its distance from Earth. The Type 1A supernova shown here is about 50 million light-years from Earth.

AFTER THE BLAST

Neutron stars and black HOLES

an imaginary neutron star outburst

A massive star's supernova is an intensely wild explosion that blasts outer shell remnants into space. But what happens to material left behind? This central core collapses in on itself so forcefully that everything gets squished together in the densest possible way. If the core's mass is between two and three times the sun's, the core material becomes a neutron star, packed into a sphere about 10 miles (16.1 km) across. When the core holds at least three times the sun's mass, the matter compresses even more, creating a black hole. To imagine how dense the core becomes in a black hole, imagine squeezing three whole suns into a ball as wide as a city on Earth.

SPACE TRAVEL ATTRACTIONS

SET YOUR WATCH BY IT
Neutron stars spin with a clocklike regularity—actually, they're more regular than clockwork! The fastest one on record turns 716 times per second.

A "NEARBY" BLACK HOLE
In the constellation Monoceros (the Unicorn) is one of Earth's closest known black holes, if not the closest: V616 Monocerotis, about 3,000 light-years away.

DO SOME HEAVY LIFTING
You would need some serious strength training before dipping into a neutron star and scooping out a teaspoon of its material. On Earth, it would weigh more than 2,300 times as much as the Empire State Building: 827 million tons (750 million t).

5 COOL FACTS TO RECORD

1 X-RAYS MARK THE SPOT
Marked by a glowing ring

Once inside a black hole's boundary, the gravitational pull is so great that nothing can exit, not even light. Yet around the absolute darkness is a bright zone. Here, material rushing toward the hole—hydrogen gas from the yellowish star to the left in this illustration—rubs against other material, heats up, and glows in different forms of light, including X-rays.

2 PULLED APART

Far from a black hole everything is normal. Closer in, its gravity is thought to have weird, extreme effects. A few inches can make a big difference in how forcefully the gravity pulls on anything—including overly adventurous astronauts in science fiction. The predicted result is a lengthwise stretching effect called spaghettification.

3 A CRAB'S PULSING HEART
Crab Nebula

Within the constellation Taurus lies the Crab Nebula, the remnant of a supernova witnessed in 1054. Inside that hides a pulsar, which is a spinning neutron star emitting a constant beam of radio waves that sweeps toward Earth with each spin. Detected on Earth, the radio signal pulses regularly.

4 THE CRAB NEBULA IN X-RAY

A glowing globe of X-rays forming the core in this image pinpoints the pulsar at the heart of the Crab Nebula. The pulsar—the white dot at the center—hurls high-energy particles that slam into material one-half light-year away. This makes the material light up in X-rays. Meanwhile, particles caught up in the star's extreme magnetism are thrust outward, appearing as jets streaming from the poles of the star.

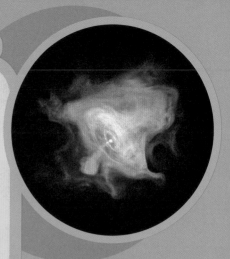

In this artist's impression of a black hole's surroundings, a disk of glowing hot gas swirls into the center, masking the dark hole from view. A high-energy jet of matter shoots from this region.

DID YOU KNOW?

There are different types of black holes. Those created during supernovas—stellar mass black holes—are the least massive and smallest known to exist. Larger, intermediate mass black holes and supermassive black holes range from 1,000 to a whopping 27 billion times the mass of our sun.

5 X-TRATERRESTRIAL VISION

Stars' remains are marvels. So are the telescopes that help us detect their secrets, such as the 32-ton (29-t) Chandra X-ray Observatory illustrated here. Located beyond Earth's X-ray absorbing atmosphere, Chandra captures and images the invisible high-energy signals that power across light-years toward Earth.

STAR CLUSTERS

star cluster Westerlund 2

Groups and globs of many STARS

1 GLOBULAR CLUSTERS
Unknown beginnings

The many reddish stars in this illustration of a typical globular cluster indicate that it hosts the galaxy's first and therefore oldest stars. However, in reality the rocky planets pictured here could be rare. The stars existed so early on, the universe may have lacked the specific materials that make up these planets.

A starry night can be breathtaking. So, too, are highly magnified views of star clusters. A cluster is a group of stars that formed from a common cloud of gas and dust at about the same time. The stars stay together because the gravity of each star pulls on the others. Open clusters are loose formations numbering from about 10 stars to 10,000. In the Milky Way, there are 1,200 of these clusters cataloged, but possibly as many as 100,000 hide behind dust. One hundred and forty-seven globular clusters are known. They are giant, spherical masses with hundreds of thousands, or even millions, of some of the oldest stars in the universe. Try finding a few the next time you peer into a star-filled sky.

2 CROWDED CORE

In this image of globular cluster M2—in the constellation Aquarius (the Water Carrier)—every dot is a star. As in all globular clusters, stars are densely packed in the core. In M2, half its mass is crammed into the core. The other half is scattered in the remaining 99 percent of the cluster. The 150,000 or so ancient stars in M2 formed about 13 billion years ago, when the universe was young and the Milky Way still forming.

SPACE TRAVEL ATTRACTIONS

➥ GIVE IT A TRY
With a star guide in hand, seek these open clusters visible with the unaided eye: the Pleiades (M45), Beehive cluster (M44), Ursa Major cluster.

➥ VISIT THE BEEHIVE
In the Beehive cluster are the first sun-like stars in such a group discovered to have planets orbiting them. If you visit, bring life support. These are uninhabitable, Jupiter-like planets.

➥ ENJOY A UNIQUE VIEW
Visiting a globular cluster? Be sure to peer inward, toward the center of the cluster, where individual stars are so close together that it may be difficult to pick them out from the brilliant glow.

DID YOU KNOW?

Many of the star clusters have names beginning with *M*. The M means that they were listed in comet-hunter Charles Messier's catalog of nebulous objects. He kept a list to avoid mistaking them for comets.

3 OPEN CLUSTERS
M7, Scorpius constellation

An open star cluster called M7 shines in the constellation Scorpius (the Scorpion). About 1,000 light-years from Earth, it is one of about 1,200 open clusters in the Milky Way. M7 is known to backyard astronomers as a brilliant, large cluster in the night sky visible to the unaided eye.

DIGITAL TRAVELER!

Watch stars fling through space as part of a computer model showing a gas cloud becoming a star cluster. (3-D glasses optional.) Search the Internet for the phrase "Large Star Cluster Formation in 3-D by Matthew Bate."

an imaginary view from a planet's cave of the night sky with a neighboring planet and globular cluster

OUR GALAXY AND BEYOND

5 GLOBULAR CLUSTER
M55, Sagittarius constellation

Light from a star on one side of the M55 cluster takes about 100 years to cross to the other side, and about 17,000 light-years to reach Earth. With binoculars, amateur astronomers enjoy its grainy, rather than cloudy, appearance, which hints at the 100,000 individual stars within.

4 GALACTIC HALO

Like bees swarming around hives, globular clusters orbit around a spiral galaxy's center. While the galaxy's arms form a flattened disk shape, the orbits of these clusters occupy a spherical space around the bulge, part of a so-called galactic halo.

halo   globular clusters

arm

ORBITING CLUSTERS

galaxy center

GALAXIES
Billions of STARS

DIGITAL TRAVELER!
To see how a galaxy evolves, go to *curiosity.com* and search for "NASA computer model shows disk galaxy life history."

O nly 100 years ago, astronomers in general figured that the Milky Way was the entire universe—everything that exists. Today, it's known as one of billions of galaxies. Each galaxy is a collection of stars and other matter, held together by gravity. Typical galaxies host millions or many billions of stars. Galactic exploration has opened a window to the larger sweep of the universe—its past, present, and possible future. With their instruments, astronomers reveal an ever changing universe, gigantic beyond imagination, and as full of questions as it is rich with galaxies.

5 COOL FACTS TO RECORD

1 SORTING BY SHAPE
Galaxy types

Galaxies come in a few basic types, each with specific shapes including elliptical, spiral, and irregular—as shown in this composite image. Some galaxies are a mix of types—for example, lenticular galaxies are a mix of spiral and elliptical. Astronomers once thought all galaxies changed gradually from elliptical to lenticular and then to spirals. Although they now think the ways galaxies form and change are more complicated than this, they still find it useful to group galaxies into these different categories.

2 ROUNDED ELLIPTICALS

At one time elliptical galaxies were thought to be the first, "baby" stage of all galaxies. They mostly have an elderly population of stars and contain less dust and gas than other galaxy types. There's not much material to support new star formation. Elliptical galaxies include some that are round or cigar-shaped.

GALAXY SHAPES

M87, an elliptical galaxy

Sombrero, a spiral galaxy

3 SEE SWIRLING SPIRALS

With thin, swirling disks of stars, gas, and dust orbiting a bright central zone, our own Milky Way is a typical spiral galaxy. New stars form mainly in the disk. While it has a central bulge of stars orbiting in random directions, not all spirals have bulges. A spiral galaxy can have a central zone with a bar-shaped mass of stars.

Andromeda, a spiral galaxy

SPACE TRAVEL ATTRACTIONS

➤ VISIT THE MANY NEIGHBORS
The Milky Way has at least 50 satellite galaxies in orbit around its center, including the two Magellanic Clouds and the Draco Dwarf galaxy.

➤ EVIDENCE OF BLACK HOLES
Signs of a supermassive black hole at the center of a galaxy include the innermost stars whizzing in tight orbits, high-energy light rings, and jets of material spewing from the galactic center.

➤ TRY TO FIND DARK MATTER
In the 1970s, astronomers discovered evidence for an unseen source of gravity that influences the motions of stars in galaxies. This "dark matter" apparently surrounds galaxies and represents most of the matter in the universe.

4 GALAXY GROUPS
Pegasus

Most galaxies don't go it alone, but end up in groups—like Stephan's Quintet in the constellation Pegasus. Just as hanging out with friends can influence you, the interactions among close galaxies can change one another. Galaxies might merge, collide, or just tug on each other, with the potential to change each other's shapes, sizes, and starmaking activities within.

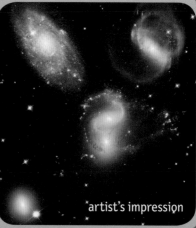

artist's impression

Constellation map labels: TRIANGULUM, LACERTA, ANDROMEDA, Stephan's Quintet, ARIES, α Scheat, β η, VULPECULA, Alpharetz, μ, Great Square, SAGITTA, HR 8799, PEGASUS, 51 Pegasi, γ Markab, DELPHINUS, Algenib, α ξ, M15, Enif ⊗, ε, PISCES, θ, EQUULEUS

Cigar, an irregular starburst galaxy

5 IRREGULAR AND LENTICULAR

Irregular galaxies are just that—they have no particular shape, and otherwise do not share much in common. Some are starburst galaxies, which, like a pan of hot popcorn kernels in action, are centers of rapid star birth. Less common are lenticular galaxies (not shown). Each is like a spiral galaxy, with a flat disk and a bulge, but a lenticular galaxy has no spiral arms, little or no interstellar material, and contains mostly old stars.

NGC 1309, a spiral arm galaxy

NGC 1300, a barred spiral galaxy

127

COLLIDING GALAXIES

Reconstruction ZONES

Smash! Crunch! When two fast cars go out of control and collide, both are usually badly damaged or destroyed. Galactic collisions are slow-motion events. Some take hundreds of millions of years. And when galaxies "collide" they pretty much pass through each other. They aren't solid. There aren't any walls that crumple. Don't expect stars to slam together, either. There's simply way too much space around them for that to happen. That may leave you wondering: What *does* happen when galaxies get so close? Read on!

⌐ WHIRLPOOL GALAXY
In glorious, natural color

This may look like a collision between two galaxies, but actually, over hundreds of millions of years, the smaller NGC 5195 galaxy (see map, right) has been moseying past the larger M51, or Whirlpool galaxy. Some astronomers think that NGC 5195's influence is constructive, helping spark new star formation (pink areas) and creating well-defined lanes in the arms of the giant Whirlpool galaxy. These galaxies lie within the two-star constellation of Canes Venatici (the Hunting Dogs)—see the sky map on page 22.

NGC 5195 • *M106*
M51 (Whirlpool Galaxy) • *Y Canum Venaticorum*
M63 • *M94* • *β*
α Cor Caroli
CANES VENATICI

DID YOU KNOW?

Some people claim our solar system migrated from the Sagittarius Dwarf galaxy during a past collision with the Milky Way. Although stars do get ripped from one galaxy to another, scientists have debunked the claim that this happened to our sun.

▸ SCORE A BULL'S-EYE
For a showy display that rivals fireworks, there's nothing like a head-on collision of two galaxies 30 million light-years from Earth.

▸ A SWEET ANALOGY
As you watch galaxies collide, imagine mixing two huge vats of cookie dough together. If each batter is mostly dough (space) around a comparatively few chocolate chips (stars), it's little wonder that no chips (stars) collide as the batters (galaxies) blend or interact.

▸ A MASS COLLISION
Head for galaxy cluster MS1054-03 where 13 collisions are taking place at the same time!

5 COOL FACTS TO RECORD

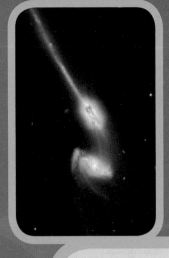

1. THE MICE GALAXIES

The bright, long galactic tail in this concept image has earned this pair of galaxies their rodent nickname. As they approach one another, each galaxy's gravity disturbs the other's material. Gas and stars are sheared from outer areas. They form streaming tails. Although the Mice galaxies will likely merge, this kind of tail can form even when galaxies simply fly by each other.

DIGITAL TRAVELER!
Galaxy flybys and collisions are always attractive events. See for yourself in a telescopic photo album of galactic encounters. Visit *spacetelescope.org/images* and search for "galaxy interactions."

WARPING GALAXIES

Scientists predict that when our Milky Way and the Andromeda galaxy plow through each other in four billion years, Earth will follow the sun as it is flung to the fringes of the Milky Way. The galaxies will warp each other and create new star zones for two billion years, ultimately merging into one. This is an artist's impression of the warp.

CARTWHEEL GALAXY

Heave a boulder into a pond and waves surge outward. Plunge a small galaxy head-on through a bigger one and energy bulldozes through the system at 200,000 miles an hour (322,000 km/h). Gas and dust scrunch up. As the compressed material collapses, new stars burst into being. Such a collision may have happened between one of the galaxies on the left of this colorized image and the larger Cartwheel galaxy on the right.

COLLIDING GALAXIES

When two galaxies "collide," their gases and dust scrunch together; new stars might form; gravity wrenches matter and stars; and sometimes the two galaxies morph into one. Here, two spiral galaxies—the top one seen edge-on, the bottom one face-on—are about to collide.

OUR GALAXY AND BEYOND

A UNIVERSE OF GALAXIES

A vat of BUBBLES

When astronauts first journeyed beyond Earth in 1968, they looked back to their home planet. The big-picture view of our place in space changed the astronauts' lives and perhaps changed humanity. If you could leave the universe and similarly look back, what would you see? Remarkably, scientists are mapping this massive area. They see ... bubbles. Not literal soap bubbles, of course, but a structure that looks like of a pan full of them. Like bubble walls, thin surfaces curve around empty spaces in an elegantly simple structure. Zoom in to see that these surfaces are groups of galaxies. Zoom in further to find one galaxy, with an ordinary star—our sun— orbited by an ordinary planet—Earth. How extraordinary.

SPACE TRAVEL ATTRACTIONS

GRAB SOME ME TIME
Feeling crowded? Cruise alone across a cosmic void—an empty area surrounded by the membranes. At light speed, you'll have 87 million years to yourself.

WALK THE WALLS
If you were to follow the longest of the universe's soap bubble membranes, or cosmic walls, at light speed, you'd travel nonstop for a billion years or more.

WRAP YOUR MIND AROUND UNIVERSE(S)
"Universe" used to mean everything. Period. But now it seems possible we cannot probe *everything*. Today, "the universe" sometimes means "the observable universe"—everything within the limits of time and place that we can possibly probe.

1 GALAXY CLUSTERS AND SUPERCLUSTERS

Gravity pulls things together—gas in stars, stars in galaxies. Galaxies gather, too, sometimes by the thousands, forming galaxy clusters and superclusters with tremendously superheated gas. This gas can be as hot as 180 million °F (82 million °C), filling space between them. These clusters hide a secret. The gravity among the galaxies isn't enough to bring them together. The source of the extra gravity is a dark secret.

2 DARK MATTER

The universe holds a mysterious source of gravity that cannot be properly explained. This unseen matter—the ghostly dark ring in this composite Hubble telescope photo—seems to pull on galaxy clusters, drawing galaxies toward it. But what is this strange stuff? It's not giant black holes, planets, stars, or antimatter. These would show themselves indirectly. For now, astronomers call this source of gravity "dark matter."

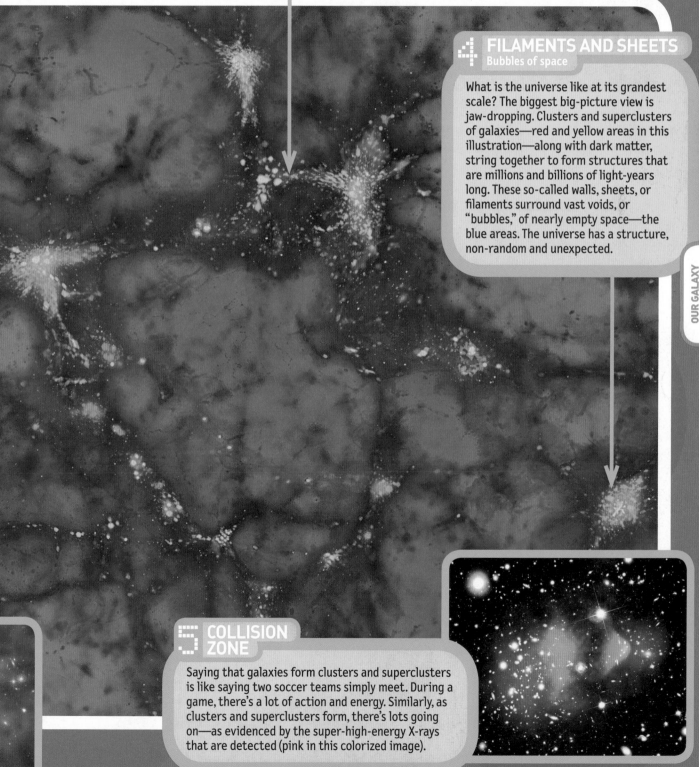

DIGITAL TRAVELER!
Take a simulated flight through our universe, thanks to the data collected by the Sloan Digital Sky Survey. Search the Internet for "APOD flight through universe sdss." Sit back and enjoy the ride!

3 IT STARTED WHEN …
The Big Bang

Long ago, the universe was compressed: It was hotter, smaller, denser than now, and completely uniform—almost. Extremely minor unevenness led to a powerful energy release that astronomers call the Big Bang. In a blip of time the universe expanded tremendously. The first particles formed. Atoms, galaxies, forces, and light … all developed from this. Today's great filaments (see fact 4) may be organized where those first uneven patches existed.

4 FILAMENTS AND SHEETS
Bubbles of space

What is the universe like at its grandest scale? The biggest big-picture view is jaw-dropping. Clusters and superclusters of galaxies—red and yellow areas in this illustration—along with dark matter, string together to form structures that are millions and billions of light-years long. These so-called walls, sheets, or filaments surround vast voids, or "bubbles," of nearly empty space—the blue areas. The universe has a structure, non-random and unexpected.

OUR GALAXY AND BEYOND

5 COLLISION ZONE

Saying that galaxies form clusters and superclusters is like saying two soccer teams simply meet. During a game, there's a lot of action and energy. Similarly, as clusters and superclusters form, there's lots going on—as evidenced by the super-high-energy X-rays that are detected (pink in this colorized image).

MAPPING SPACE

Plotting in multiple DIMENSIONS

Maps of space show the relative positions of planets, stars, galaxies, and other objects. They also help us navigate. The simplest ones— two-dimensional maps such as the sky charts on pages 20–27—display how objects' locations relate in east-west and north-south directions. A three-dimensional map adds depth, providing information about what is above or below the east-west-north-south plane. (Similar to the illustration on pages 32–33.) Time adds a fourth dimension to maps, showing, for instance, how things change or move. Additional details are added in as layers of information. For example, a map might use a color code to show temperature in different locations on a planet. These types of maps help astronomers seek out and notice patterns in space, visualizing the universe and aiding space exploration.

AUNT BERTHA'S
SPACE TRAVEL TIPS

You can print out free star maps at *skymaps.com* to match and identify stars. There are different maps for the Northern and Southern Hemispheres.

Join a local astronomy group or club to learn more about mapping the night sky. For details, go to *skyandtelescope.com*.

If you're using an ordinary compass in space, remember the needle will be influenced not by Earth's magnetic field but by whatever magnetic effects might be caused by streaming particles and the magnetism of moons, planets, or stars where you are.

Here are 6 of a total of 66 giant antennas, or radio wave collecting dishes, forming the Atacama Large Millimeter Array radio telescope in northern Chile. The telescope is used mainly to learn about how planets and stars form, but its ability to see far out into the universe helps astronomers map the night sky.

MAPPING SPACE

WHERE ARE WE?

A history of Earth's position in SPACE

microwave radiation colorized sky map

DIGITAL TRAVELER!
To find out more about astrolabes and to learn about related instruments known as orreries, search the Internet for "How to use an astrolabe video" and "LEGO Orrery—Earth, Moon and Sun."

People have been investigating space for ages, but what we see and how we interpret it has changed. Early civilizations associated the movements of planets and stars with the work of their gods. In ancient Greece, many astronomers thought Earth was at the center of the universe. This view was widely held in the West until the observations and careful thinking of astronomers Nicolaus Copernicus, Galileo Galilei, and Johannes Kepler proved that it was incorrect. Ever more powerful telescopes and new observations of other galaxies, exoplanets, and evidence for an ever changing universe have led to new maps of space that continue to transform how people view our place in the universe.

5 COOL FACTS TO RECORD

DID YOU KNOW?

The fictional odysseys of *Star Trek* TV have led creators to make a *Star Trek* atlas of the Milky Way. Maps include Sol system's planet Sol III—Earth—and Beta Quadrant's Klingon Empire.

1 THE SEASONS AND THE SUN

This structure in Britain was arranged so that some of the massive stones line up with the sun at sunrise and sunset on the longest and shortest days of the year. These days are called the summer and winter solstices (see page 11). This monumental 4,500-year-old stone circle, Stonehenge, is an impressive reminder of the importance of sky knowledge to early civilizations.

2 BUILDING UP A PICTURE

Stars and galaxies send out streams of radiation. Scientists record the radiation to create space maps. This oval gamma-ray image of the whole sky was created over six years. The brighter the color, the higher the energy of the gamma-ray signals. The horizontal line is an edge-on view of the flat disk of the Milky Way galaxy.

3 CELESTIAL ATLAS

In the 1600s, recently invented telescopes were used to help create star maps. These creations were also works of art. Compare this 1661 map of the Southern Hemisphere constellations and signs of the zodiac to the modern maps on pages 24–27 of this atlas.

4 NAVIGATING BY THE STARS

By the mid-800s A.D., Arab astronomers had developed instruments for plotting the positions of stars in the sky and determining time and locations on Earth. This circular astrolabe is a device for measuring star positions. Its viewing sights (at the end of each long arm) hint at its function.

5 EGYPTIAN EYES ON THE SKY

Attuned to the sky, the ancient Egyptians marked the movements of five planets and numerous constellations, and were the first to set a yearly solar calendar at 365 days. This art from approximately 3,000 years ago illustrates the earth god Geb on the ground while the air god Shu raises Nut, the sky goddess (the large, arched figure), above him.

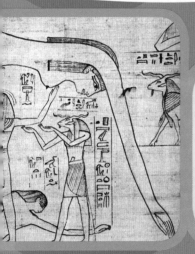

SKYWATCH

Exploration around the WORLD

planetarium in
Moscow, Russia

Worldwide, over time, curious peoples have created places dedicated to observing and exploring space. Today, you can explore these places as part of your astronomical journey. Observatories, rocket launch sites, command and control centers, and science museums share artifacts and engaging experiences. Various national space agencies offer websites with news, maps, photographs, and videos. Sixty or so Dark Sky Places dotting the globe offer opportunities for sky gazers to peer into uniquely deep, dark, night skies filled with countless stars.

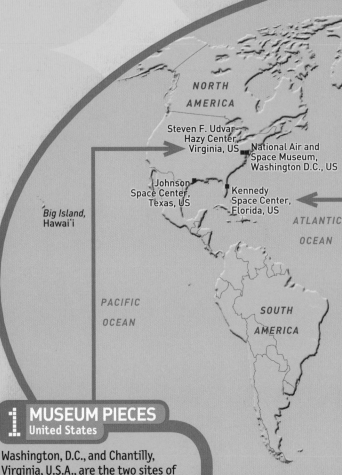

NORTH
AMERICA

Steven F. Udvar-
Hazy Center,
Virginia, US

National Air and
Space Museum,
Washington D.C., US

Johnson
Space Center,
Texas, US

Kennedy
Space Center,
Florida, US

Big Island,
Hawai'i

ATLANTIC

OCEAN

PACIFIC
OCEAN

SOUTH
AMERICA

SPACE TRAVEL
ATTRACTIONS

▶ LISTENING TO RADIO SIGNALS
Tune in to radio astronomy at the world's largest radio telescope in Guizhou Province, China. The recently completed bowl-shaped radio wave antenna stretches 1,642 feet (500 m) across.

▶ HOUSTON TO BASE
Johnson Space Center in Houston, Texas, U.S.A., is NASA's mission control and education site for space exploration. Visit the center or its website to learn about moon landings, the International Space Station (ISS), and the space shuttle.

▶ ISLAND OBSERVATORY
Visit the summit of Mauna Kea on Hawaii's Big Island to stargaze and see the world's largest array of big optical telescopes.

1 MUSEUM PIECES
United States

Washington, D.C., and Chantilly, Virginia, U.S.A., are the two sites of the Smithsonian's National Air and Space Museum, home to a large collection of significant space artifacts. Highlights include the Apollo 11 command module *Columbia*, space shuttle orbiter vehicle *Discovery*, and a full-scale mock-up of the Hubble Space Telescope.

2 WHERE TIME BEGINS
United Kingdom

The Royal Observatory at Greenwich in Britain was opened in 1676. In the late 1800s, the Greenwich, or Prime, Meridian—0° longitude—was set here. This imaginary line is the "starting point" for international time zones and divides Earth into Eastern and Western Hemispheres.

3 VIEWING THE SUN
Russia

The Solar Radio Telescope at Badary in Russia consists of an array of dishes used to analyze the sun's activity. Combining its data with that of other solar telescopes, scientists can map the sun's magnetic field and radiation.

ARCTIC OCEAN

Royal Observatory Greenwich, UK

Badary Radio Astronomical Observatory, Russia

EUROPE

ASIA

AFRICA

Jantar Mantar, India

Guizhou Province, China

PACIFIC OCEAN

INDIAN OCEAN

AUSTRALIA

ANTARCTICA

■ Astronomical point of interest

0 —— 2000 miles
0 —— 2000 kilometers

4 SIMPLE OBSERVATIONS
India

The Jantar Mantar is an astronomical observation site at Jaipur, India, built in the early 1700s. It has a set of about 20 fixed instruments, used to study the day and night sky with the naked eye. These include sundials to tell the time and date and astrolabes to monitor the constellations.

MAPPING SPACE

5 PREPARE FOR TAKEOFF
United States

The Kennedy Space Center in Florida, U.S.A., an active rocket launch base and assembly site, welcomes visitors at its Visitor Complex. You can see exhibits and displays related to rockets, satellites, and human spaceflight since the 1960s.

SCANNING THE SKIES

Searching for the almost INVISIBLE

Light makes the universe visible to our human eyes. Hot objects send out, or radiate, their own light. Other objects bounce, or reflect, any light that strikes them from other sources. We can't see all of this light, but technology can help expand our vision. Optical telescopes make faint and distant light sources seem brighter and closer. Other telescopes detect and process forms of light energy we cannot see, such as infrared light, invisible radio waves, X-rays, and gamma rays. Color-coded, colorized images can pinpoint where these energy sources have been detected. Whether on the ground or in space, increasingly sensitive telescopes help us map an ever more detailed universe.

SPACE TRAVEL ATTRACTIONS

GLASS EYES
When light enters a glass lens, the light's path bends, or refracts. Pairs of lenses in binoculars and some optical telescopes, called refractors, are specially shaped and positioned to bend light for magnification.

REFLECTED GLORIES
Optical reflector telescopes use arranged mirrors instead of lenses to change the path of incoming light. Light streams into the telescope, strikes mirrors, and bounces, or reflects, off their surfaces to create magnified images.

TUNING IN
An antenna of a radio telescope, often a bowl-shaped reflecting dish, focuses signals from space and directs them to a receiver. The receiver serves as a detector and links to computers that record and analyze the signals.

DID YOU KNOW?

Radiation from space comes in many forms. Some include visible light that we can see with our eyes, and gamma rays, X-rays, ultraviolet light, infrared waves, microwaves, and radio waves. To find out about radiation from the Big Bang, go online to research "cosmic microwave background radiation."

COOL FACTS TO RECORD

1 HUBBLE SPACE TELESCOPE
High above Earth's atmosphere, the Hubble Space Telescope orbits Earth every 97 minutes. It was delivered into space by a space shuttle in 1990. This reflecting telescope has provided data that inform scientific understanding of the universe's formation and age. It has also confirmed the existence of dark energy, the mysterious energy that makes the universe continuously expand.

2 A LARGE REFLECTOR
The power of the 4- and 8.5-foot (1.25- and 2.6-m)-wide optical telescopes at the Crimean Astrophysical Observatory in Ukraine help astronomers detect minor planets and asteroids and investigate the structure and formation of stars and galaxies. Each reflector is housed in a dome with a viewing slit that has a retractable cover.

138

TELESCOPE ARRAY

Most modern radio telescopes consist of not one but many steerable antennas. One such telescope is located at the Combined Array for Research in Millimeter-wave Astronomy, or CARMA, near Los Angeles, California, U.S.A. Its 23 antennas have been used together, acting like one, giant telescope miles (km) across in size. With CARMA, astronomers study early planet formation and star birth, supernovas, and galactic mergers.

BACKYARD EXPERT

Stargazers, astronomers, or anyone interested in the night sky can see and learn a lot about space using binoculars, small reflectors, refractors, and even smartphones and tablets. Viewing is best far from city lights on a clear night when there is little or no cloud cover.

DETECTING GRAVITY WAVES

Wham! More than one billion years ago, two black holes collided. This caused ripples throughout space called gravitational waves. On Earth, on September 14, 2015, some of these waves disturbed two precise arrangements of crisscrossed laser beams in steel tubes that stretched for miles (km). When both sets of beams wobbled, scientists celebrated the first ever detection of gravity waves.

MAPPING SPACE

139

MACHINES IN SPACE

Escaping Earth's ATMOSPHERE

Three, two, one—blastoff! A rocket shoots out gas, the gas pushes back, and a rocket with its cargo launches forward. To go into space, the rocket's send-off requires a thrust, or push, great enough to reach a swift 25,031 miles an hour (40,283 km/h). This "escape velocity" is the outward speed required to overcome the pull of Earth's gravity. Spacecraft and instruments such as satellites, shuttles, and most space telescopes require only a partial escape. Rocketed at less than escape velocity, they end up circling, or orbiting, Earth. Gravity keeps them close to home. Whether in orbit or beyond, space machines open up a universe of information to those of us watching on the ground.

5 COOL FACTS TO RECORD

SPACE TRAVEL ATTRACTIONS

➥ STEERING A WAY INTO SPACE
Watch a rocket as it takes off. Look at the rear end for the steerable engine nozzles that can be pointed slightly to one side to turn the vehicle in the sky.

➥ BURNING UP
Rockets are fitted with boosters that burn fuel for a few minutes to create a surge of thrust before falling away. Early rockets had boosters that fell to Earth as waste, but some newer ones have reusable boosters.

➥ GRAVITY SLINGSHOTS
In a maneuver called a gravity assist, space probes use the gravity of objects such as the sun or planets to change their speed of travel and to change direction.

1 SATELLITES IN ORBIT

Artificial satellites continuously orbit Earth at various heights and speeds, providing data for communication, navigation, mapping, and monitoring weather and natural resources on Earth. This Fermi Gamma-ray Space Telescope is an orbiting observatory. Equipped with solar panels for power, it is used to observe energy emitted from the regions near distant black holes.

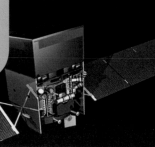

2 WORKING IN SPACE

Conducting repairs during an extra vehicular activity (EVA), or space walk, is one duty of space station astronauts. They also run experiments in station laboratories, including investigating the effects of long-term spaceflights on the body. This paves the way for human missions to Mars and beyond.

3 LAUNCH TO A SPACE LAB

Space stations provide long-term housing aboard space-based laboratories orbiting Earth. The International Space Station has housed astronauts continuously for more than 15 years. China's Tiangong program involves a series of space stations. Here, a capsule on a Chinese CZ-2F rocket awaits lift-off for a 2011 docking test with Tiangong 1, which was occupied briefly in 2012 and 2013. In September 2016, China launched an orbital module as part of space station Tiangong 2.

5 LANDING ON ITS FEET

As their name suggests, landers are craft or instruments that land on objects in space in order to study them close-up. To date, landers have studied the moon, Venus, Mars, Titan, an asteroid, and a comet. In 2005, the car-size lander Huygens was parachuted onto the surface of Titan, Saturn's largest moon. It sent images to Earth for 90 minutes before its batteries ran out of power.

4 ROBOTIC ROVERS

These landers travel the surface of space objects. They are fitted with such instruments as cameras, rock drilling equipment, atmosphere and soil analysis instruments, and a power source—perhaps solar panels or a radioactive material. The ExoMars Rover shown here is due to be sent to Mars in 2018. Its mission: search for possible signs of life on the planet.

141

5 COOL FACTS TO RECORD

1 LOOK THROUGH A TELESCOPE

Your school, a library, a local astronomy club, or an amateur astronomer may have a small, high-quality professional telescope you can use. As you enjoy the satisfaction of observing sky objects firsthand, try to imagine what it must have been like for the first telescope users, who had no idea what they were about to discover.

2 USING SMART DEVICES

Try some of the many astronomy apps available for your smartphone or computer tablet. You can use them to gather news and images from NASA, track satellites and the ISS, hear the latest about extraterrestrial happenings, or see an annotated star map of the part of the sky you are viewing. Many astronomy apps are free.

binoculars

3 BINOCULAR VISION

Binoculars will show you a broader sweep of sky than most telescopes, while still magnifying targets. Try viewing the moon, the planets, and star clusters such as the Pleiades through a low-power pair. Enjoy the Milky Way, but also view a nearby galaxy— Andromeda or a Magellanic Cloud, depending on your hemisphere.

telescope

smartphone and tablet

142

BACKYARD OBSERVATION

4 VISIT A PLANETARIUM

Immersed in the deep dark of a planetarium, you might just forget you are indoors, looking at projections on a dome-shaped screen. Planets, stars, and galaxies seem real. Sitting under the dome, peer into deep space, learn how space objects move, or zoom in on destinations throughout the universe.

Amateur ASTRONOMERS

This book's imaginary trek through space is winding down, but your space adventures can continue. You might revisit the pages' astronomical images, but also try experiencing astronomy firsthand. Start simply. Step outside. Look up—no telescope required. Over weeks, watch the moon, stars, or patterns in the sky that stand out. Can you spot any planets "wandering" across the stellar background, or meteors and artificial satellites passing overhead? Public astronomy programs, exhibits, books, magazines, and websites can help you learn more. Enjoy the journey!

5 WITH THE NAKED EYE

In the night sky, can you find satellites, Venus, details on the moon, meteors, comets, the Milky Way, auroras, and constellations? Some are visible most nights, others only rarely. As you gaze, remember that you are continuing a practice that has inspired human hearts and minds for thousands of years.

SPACE TRAVEL ATTRACTIONS

ORIENT YOURSELF
The night sky appears different in the Northern and Southern Hemispheres. Remember to check the time of year on a sky map (such as those on pages 20–27).

TAKE YOUR TIME
On a dark night, it can take as long as 30 minutes for your eyes to get used to very low light levels. Take something comfortable to sit on while your eyes adjust.

RECORD YOUR OBSERVATIONS
Sharp astronomers write down and photograph or sketch what they see. Note the time, date, year, and location of your observations.

MAPPING SPACE

SIGNS OF THE ZODIAC

Star patterns in the night SKY

SPACE TRAVEL ATTRACTIONS

Today, astronomers officially recognize 88 constellations. In ancient times, constellations related to the sun were the most significant. Watching this bright sphere, early people noticed its position shifting gradually over the year in a set pattern. For example, each morning in northern winter through spring, the sun rises a bit farther north than on the day before. Even so, it stays within a narrow range of sky that also includes a band of constellations. Watching these 12 constellations—the zodiac—today puts us in touch with a long human tradition.

CELESTIAL SPHERE
Looking at star patterns that followed the sun's path in the sky, ancient Greeks saw several animals, calling this set of constellations a "circle of animals," or, in Greek, *zodiac*. As you can see, however, not all zodiacal constellations are animals.

SPOT THE CONSTELLATION
Look at the 12 constellations of the zodiac shown here, then locate them—and others— on the sky maps shown on pages 20 to 27 of this book. The "Look for it" dates will give you the best chances of seeing the constellations. You may not be able to spot all of the stars.

IT'S ALL GREEK AND LATIN
Most of the names of the northern constellations were given by ancient Greek astronomers or early celestial mapmakers who used Latin names.

ASTROLOGY
Quite separate from the science of astronomy, astrology is based on ancient, pre-scientific beliefs—including the idea that a person's life is influenced by which zodiacal constellation aligns, or lines up, with the sun on his or her birth date.

ARIES
Meaning of name: the Ram
Try to see: 4 stars
Look for it: October–November

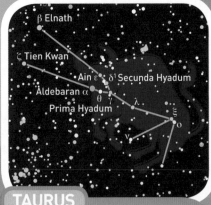

TAURUS
Meaning of name: the Bull
Try to see: 10 stars
Look for it: November–December

GEMINI
Meaning of name: the Twins
Try to see: 16 stars
Look for it: January–February

CANCER
Meaning of name: the Crab
Try to see: 5 stars
Look for it: January–March

LEO
Meaning of name: the Lion
Try to see: 9 stars
Look for it: February–April

VIRGO
Meaning of name: the Maiden
Try to see: 11 stars
Look for it: April–May

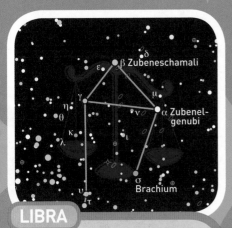

LIBRA
Meaning of name: the Scales
Try to see: 4 stars
Look for it: June

SCORPIUS
Meaning of name: the Scorpion
Try to see: 14 stars
Look for it: July

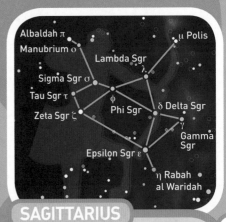

SAGITTARIUS
Meaning of name: the Archer
Try to see: 12 stars
Look for it: mid-July–mid-August

CAPRICORNUS
Meaning of name: the Sea Goat
Try to see: 9 stars
Look for it: mid-August–mid-October

AQUARIUS
Meaning of name: the Water Carrier
Try to see: 14 stars
Look for it: October–mid-November

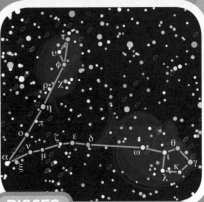

PISCES
Meaning of name: the Fish
Try to see: 12 stars
Look for it: November–December

A NEW ATLAS

Stepping into a space FUTURE

I n the past 100 years, science has changed our understanding of the universe. Thanks to ever more powerful telescopes, rockets, and spacecraft, our ability to probe the depths of space and time has surged. What's next? Expect to witness the first human steps on Mars, which may lead toward extraterrestrial colonies and mining in space. Robotic explorers may find life on gas giants' moons, telescopes might reveal life signs on exoplanets, and scientists may resolve some mysteries of black holes, dark matter, and dark energy. Humankind's "Atlas of Space" will continue as a work in progress.

5 COOL FACTS TO RECORD

1 ENGINEERING PLANETS

Could Earthlings change the surface and atmosphere of Mars into something like the landscape and atmosphere of Earth? Some future-minded people hope that measures such as adding bacteria to the Martian soil, seeding any clouds to promote rainfall, irrigation, and other technologies might work, if only over thousands of years. Maybe this dream reveals a human desire to be at home wherever we may be in the universe.

2 OVERCOMING OBSTACLES
Designed for living

For humans in long-term zero or low gravity environments, muscles waste and bones weaken. Beyond Earth's protective atmosphere, astronauts' bodies are exposed to bombardment by highly damaging, energetic, spacecraft-penetrating cosmic and solar radiation. We must overcome these problems as we prepare to launch humans on grand odysseys into space.

4 NEW SPACECRAFT

How might we fuel long, human journeys into space? Engineers and scientists envision nuclear fusion–powered spaceships that could reach speeds of up to 600 million miles an hour (966 million km/h). A more out-there concept: Use antimatter! Extremely rare—and challenging to make—antimatter is like ordinary matter, but with some opposite characteristics. When it comes into contact with ordinary matter, enormous power is generated.

3 IMAGINING MORE UNIVERSES
Black hole connection

While we survey and explore the observable universe, some scientists sketch out possible, additional universes, perhaps with different laws of physics and more than the four dimensions of forward-backward, left-right, up-down, and time. Some wonder if black holes may lead to these proposed universes.

5 MINING ASTEROIDS
Using available materials

Will you or someone you know have an asteroid as part of your address someday? The farther from Earth people explore, the more we will need to tap into space-based resources. Possibly, people and robots will mine asteroids for metals and water ice—which can provide materials for objects, fuel, and life support. Maybe, after adapting hollowed-out asteroids, people could move in to them.

To Infinity ... and Beyond !

1 **What travels exactly 186,282 miles (299,792 km) a second?**

a. a comet
b. a spacecraft
c. light
d. an asteroid

2 **What is the record number of days spent in space by a human?**

a. 2
b. 28
c. 878
d. 1,825

3 **How many Earths could fit inside Jupiter?**

a. more than 1,000
b. 17
c. 200
d. 2

4 **Which is the farthest distance any human has ever been from Earth?**

a. 6.6 miles (11 km)
b. 23 miles (37 km)
c. 1,324 miles (2,131 km)
d. 248,655 miles (400,171 km)

5 **How old was the oldest person to ever travel in space?**

a. 24 years old
b. 53 years old
c. 77 years old
d. 101 years old

6 **How long would it take to get to Mars on a modern spacecraft?**

a. 25 days, if the traffic's not bad
b. 150 to 300 days, depending on how close Earth is to Mars
c. a little over 10 years
d. 23 years, with the right kind of rocket

7 **How long did it take for Apollo 11—the first spacecraft to land on the moon—to reach the moon?**

a. 3 days
b. 1 month
c. 1 week
d. 1 year

8 **When daredevil Felix Baumgartner skydived from the edge of Earth's atmosphere and parachuted back to Earth, about how far did he travel?**

a. 24 miles (39 km)
b. 432 miles (695 km)
c. 5,728 miles (9,218 km)
d. to infinity

9 **What is the longest amount of time spent by a human on the moon?**

a. 34 minutes
b. about 75 hours
c. 8 hours
d. 5 days

10 **True or false? Up to 98 percent of astronauts' urine can get recycled back into drinking water on the International Space Station.**

11 **About how wide was the asteroid that may have led to the dinosaurs' extinction?**

a. as wide as a soccer goal, about 24 feet (7.3 m)
b. as wide as five football fields, about 500 yards (457 m)
c. as wide as 26 Great Pyramids of Egypt, about 6 miles (10 km)
d. as wide as Taiwan, about 106 to 186 miles (171 to 299 km)

12 **What is the record for the longest human space walk?**

a. 32 minutes
b. 8 hours 56 minutes
c. 24 hours
d. 72 hours 45 minutes

A STARRY SHOW

1 What **causes** the magnificent light **show** of the northern lights, called the **aurora borealis**?

a. solar wind streams
b. exploding stars
c. black holes
d. solar eclipses

2 Which **planet** is Earth's closest **neighbor**?

a. Mercury   c. Saturn
b. Venus   d. Neptune

3 True or false? The same constellations are always seen in the **sky** from the **same** location.

4 True or false? There is a **constellation** in the sky that has a pattern of stars like a **hunter**.

5 The **millions** of tiny pieces of trash and debris floating around in Earth's atmosphere were caused by _____.

a. satellite explosions and collisions
b. astronaut garbage
c. launched space vehicles
d. all of the above

6 **Which** is the last stage of the **life** cycle of most stars?

a. nebula   c. protostar
b. white dwarf d. red giant

7 When **gazing** at the night sky, what do **people** often mistake for stars?

a. helicopters
b. planets and satellites
c. asteroids and meteors
d. the moon

8 On what area of Earth's **surface** can you see the most **stars** in the sky?

a. suburban towns
b. big cities
c. large wilderness areas
d. any rooftop

9 What **causes** the shadows and shapes we can see on the **moon**?

a. weather on Earth
b. the man on the moon
c. cheese
d. craters

10 True or False? Stars can be seen from Earth in the entire **Northern Hemisphere** every night of the year.

11 In 2004, scientists discovered a star made of _____.

a. gold   c. dust
b. carbon   d. salt

12 On which **planet** is a day—the amount of time it takes for a **planet** to rotate on its axis—longer than 200 Earth days?

a. Venus   c. Jupiter
b. Mercury   d. Uranus

13 What object(s) in the sky did **sailors** use to **navigate** ships?

a. the moon   c. constellations
b. the sun   d. all of the above

14 What **tool** do people use to get the best view of the **moon** and **stars** in the sky?

a. telescope
b. microscope
c. binoculars
d. glasses

CHECK YOUR ANSWERS ON PAGE 160.

Lost in Space

The Moon Rock concert just ended, but now these aliens can't find their spaceships in the parking lot. To help each alien locate its spaceship, follow these rules:

- Aliens with antennae need ships with pointed roofs.

- Short aliens need ladders to reach the doors of their ships.

- The number of windows on the spaceship must match the number of eyeballs on the alien.

- Purple aliens must return to the Purple Planet in purple spaceships.

THANKS FOR COMING!

EXIT

MOON-ROCK-A-THON!

Galaxy's Child Moon tour 2004

space

1.

2.

4.

5.

6.

7.

A

GLOSSARY

(includes several scientists, missions, and probes from space history that are mentioned in this book)

Apollo U.S. manned moon landing program, 1962–1973

asteroid belt the band of asteroids between Mars and Jupiter; most of the solar system's asteroids are currently thought to be in this band

asteroids rocky objects smaller than planets, formed in the early stage of the solar system

astronomers scientists who study space objects and energy

astronomical unit (AU) the average distance between the sun and Earth; one AU is equivalent to precisely 92,955,807 miles (149,597,871 km)

atmosphere the gases surrounding a space object

atom a tiny building block of matter, composed of even smaller particles called electrons and a central part called a nucleus or atomic nucleus

atomic nucleus the central part of an atom, heavier than an electron, that usually contains two small types of particles, protons and neutrons

aurora light shining in the atmosphere of a space object such as a planet, caused when high-energy particles collide with the atmosphere's particles, making them glow

Big Bang the current scientific explanation of our universe's beginning, involving a sudden change from something small, hot, and dense to something bigger, cooler, and more spread out

billion one thousand million: in figures, 1,000,000,000

binary star a system of two stars orbiting a common point

black hole a place in space with extremely intense gravity from which light cannot escape; also considered an object with the same qualities

Cassini U.S. space probe/orbiter, the first craft to orbit Saturn: launched 1997, mission ongoing

celestial sphere the region surrounding Earth in which all space objects exist; the imaginary ball-shaped form that appears to have all space objects on it

comet a frozen object made of ice and dust with an orbit that takes it close to the sun, often causing material to vaporize and leave a trail (called a tail) behind it

constellation one of 88 star patterns in the sky recognized by astronomers

Copernicus, Nicolaus Polish astronomer (1473–1543) who wrote that planets orbit the sun, not Earth

core the innermost part of an object

corona the sun's outermost atmosphere

crater a surface feature of a rocky space object appearing as a circular or elongated depression

crust the solid, outermost layer of a solid space object

dark matter invisible material that neither emits nor reflects light of any type but is known to exist because of its gravitational effect on space objects

deep-sky object any very distant item in space, including nebulas, star clusters, and galaxies

density the compactness of an object; a property determined by the amount of mass in a sample of a given size

dwarf planet a small space object that (1) orbits the sun, (2) has a round shape, (3) is not a moon, and (4) has other objects nearby and within its orbit

eclipse the passing of one space object in front of another, blocking light from the more distant object

ecliptic the apparent path of the sun on the celestial sphere

element a type of chemical such as hydrogen and helium; each element has a unique type of atom

exoplanet a planet that orbits a star other than our sun

extraterrestrial originating outside Earth

fusion joining of the nuclei of atoms, often with high release of energy

galaxy a large collection of stars held together by gravity

Galilei, Galileo Italian astronomer (1564–1642), credited as the first person to use a telescope to view space

gamma rays a kind of high-energy, invisible light

gas giant any of the outer solar system planets currently or in the past thought to be composed mainly of hydrogen and helium gases (Jupiter, Saturn, Uranus, Neptune)

globular cluster a dense collection of stars that forms a rounded shape

gravity the force that pulls matter toward other matter; this force keeps planets in orbit around a star

Halley, Edmond British scientist and mathematician (1656–1742) who was the first to calculate a comet's orbit

helium the second lightest, second most common type of atom in the universe

Hubble, Edwin American astronomer (1889–1953) whose work confirmed the existence of galaxies beyond the Milky Way

Hubble Space Telescope large U.S. reflecting telescope in Earth's orbit; launched 1990, ongoing

hydrogen the lightest and most common type of atom in the universe; main material of stars

impact a strike or hit by an object, often creating a depression or crater

infrared a kind of low-energy, invisible light, often felt as heat

inner planets the four rocky planets closest to the sun (Mercury, Venus, Earth, Mars)

interstellar between stars

invisible light a kind of energy of the same form as visible light but with higher or lower energy levels and undetectable to the human eye

Kepler U.S. space telescope mission to search for exoplanets; launched 2009, it is ongoing.

Kepler, Johannes German astronomer (1571–1630) who discovered laws of planetary motion around the central sun

Kuiper, Gerard P. American astronomer (1905–73) who helped predict the Kuiper belt's existence and after whom the belt is named

Kuiper belt a doughnut-shaped region that begins just beyond the orbit of Neptune, where there are many icy objects in orbit around the sun

lava molten (hot and melted) rock from the interior of a planet or other large, rocky space object

light a particular form of energy that travels by waves; includes visible and invisible light

light pollution any unwanted artificial light; the haze or glare that washes out views of the night sky, caused by artificial lighting

light-year the distance light can travel through an otherwise totally empty space in one year; it equals 5,878,625,373,184 miles (9,460,730,472,581 km)

magnitude a star's brightness

mantle a layer between the crust and the core of a space object

mass the total matter in an object

matter the substance, or stuff, everything is made of

MESSENGER U.S. spacecraft sent to study Mercury, 2004–15

Messier, Charles French astronomer (1730–1817) who was the first to catalog nebulas and star clusters

meteor a meteoroid as it travels through any atmosphere and leaves a streak of light as it burns up; sometimes the streak of light caused by this.

meteorite a piece of a meteoroid that falls to Earth (or to any planet, moon, and such)

meteoroid a particle, piece, or large chunk of rock traveling in space that is smaller than an asteroid

microwave a kind of low-energy, invisible light

Milky Way the large spiral galaxy that contains our solar system; traditionally, the band of stars in the night sky that are part of the galaxy seen edge-on

molecule any two or more atoms chemically bound together

molten melted by extreme heat and/or pressure

moon a natural satellite of a planet

nebula (1) anything cloudlike, (2) a large cloud of mostly gas in space, or (3) fuzzy light patches (seen mostly through telescopes), some of which are now known to be galaxies

neutron star a small, extremely compacted star, composed mostly of particles called neutrons

nucleus atomic nucleus; the central part of an atom, composed of at least one proton and usually at least one neutron

Oort cloud an enormous region of space around our solar system containing mainly icy objects such as comets

orbit the regular path of one space object around another, such as the Earth's orbit around the sun

photosphere the only layer of the sun (or any star) that releases visible light; sometimes called its surface

planet a large, round object that orbits a star in a path free of space debris

planetary nebula the shell of gas puffed off by a type of star called a red giant

pulsar a rapidly spinning neutron star that emits regular pulses of radio waves

radiate to be an initial source of light energy or to emit light energy; in contrast to "reflect"

radiation in astronomy, energy emitted from a space object such as a star; light is a form of radiation

radio waves a kind of low-energy, invisible light

red dwarf faint star about half the size of our sun, cool compared to many stars

red giant an aging, low-mass star expanded greatly from its original size, with a temperature that is cool (compared to other stars' temperatures)

reflect to redirect light after being struck by it

rocky planet a planet with a solid surface, or crust, primarily composed of minerals; a terrestrial planet; in our solar system Mercury, Venus, Earth, or Mars

rotation period the time a space object takes to spin, or turn around, once

satellite any object orbiting a planet, whether artificial (human-made) or natural, for example a moon

solar flare a sudden violent explosion of energy that occurs in the sun's atmosphere

solar nebula the cloud of dust and gas from which our sun and solar system formed

solar prominence an arc of gas between two sunspots

solar system the sun and all the space objects in orbit around it

solar wind a stream of high-energy particles from the sun or any star

space the region beyond Earth, often said to begin at 62 miles (100 km) above Earth's surface, in the thermosphere

spiral galaxy galaxy with a pinwheel shape

Sputnik several Soviet satellites that orbited Earth— Sputnik 1 was the world's first artificial satellite; 1957–1960

star a hot, giant, glowing ball of gas and gaslike material

sun the star that is the center of our solar system

sunspot a temporary dark area on the sun's surface marking the location of a magnetic storm

supergiant a very massive, bright star with a short life span

supernova the sudden, extremely energetic end of some stars that includes a huge explosion

ultraviolet a high-energy, invisible form of light; the form of light that causes a sunburn (among other things)

variable star a star whose visible light appears to change in intensity

Venera several Soviet space probes sent to Venus, with some landing on the surface; 1960s to 1980s

Viking 1 and 2 two U.S. robotic landers sent to study Mars; 1975–1982

Voyager 1 and 2 two U.S space probes exploring the outer solar system; both launched 1977, mission ongoing

white dwarf the very hot, white, final phase of some stars, such as our sun

X-rays a kind of high-energy, invisible light

INDEX

Photo Credits
Key: CO = Corbis; DR = Dreamstime; GI = Getty Images; JHU = Johns Hopkins University; SPL = Science Photo Library; SS = Shutterstock

Aunt Bertha illustration by Joe Rocco.
Cover (Earth), David Aguilar; (Mars Rover), NASA/JPL; (satellite), Andrey Armyagov/SS; (spiral galaxy), NASA; (shuttle launch), Mikephotos/DR; (Saturn), David Aguilar; (space walker), NASA; (sun), Triff/SS; (telescope), Dave Yoder/GI; (metal texture), Phiseksit/SS; back cover (Jupiter), David Aguilar; (astronaut), NASA; (Carnia), NASA, ESA, and the Hubble SM4 ERO Team; **Front matter:** 2 (CTR LE), Igor Zubkis/SS; 2 (CTR RT), JPL-Caltech/MSSS/NASA; 3 (CTR RT), Matthias Kulka/CO UK; 3 (LO CTR), X-ray: CXC/SAO/NASA; Optical: STScI/NASA; Infrared: JPL-Caltech/Steward/O. Krause et al/NASA; **Sky-High:** 6-7 (Background), Arctic-Images/CO UK; 9 (RT UP), NASA; 9 (RT CTR), Roger Ressmeyer/CO UK; 9 (RT LO), stevecoleimages/GI; 10 (UP), Corbis Historical/CO UK; 11 (UP RT), Michele Cornelius/DR; 11 (LO), SPL/CO UK; 12 (UP), Roger Ressmeyer/CO UK; 14 (LO LE), Imaginechina/CO UK; 15 (CTR), Roger Ressmeyer/CO UK; 15 (RT), NASA; 15 (LO), Larry W. Smith/epa/CO UK; 15 (LE), Roger Ressmeyer/CO UK; **Observing Space:** 16-17 (Background), Zhasmina Ivanova/DR; 18 (UP LE), Yganko/SS; 18 (CTR RT), Larry Landolfi/SPL; 28-29 (UP), JPL-Caltech/NASA; 28 (CTR RT), Hubble/NASA/ESA; 28 (LO LE), JPL-Caltech/T. Pyle (SSC)/NASA; 29 (CTR), MSFC/Meteoroid Environment Office/Bill Cooke/NASA; 29 (LO), M. Jee and H. Ford (JHU)/NASA/ESA; 31 (UP LE), Joel Kowsky/NASA; 32 (CTR LE), NOAA/GOES Project/NASA; 33 (UP RT), NASA; **Inner Solar System:** 34-35 (Background), NASA - digital version copyright/Science Faction/CO UK; 36 (UP LE), Roger Ressmeyer/CO UK; 36 (UP RT), Susazoom/DR; 36 (LO RT), SDO/NASA; 37 (Background), NASA/CO UK; 37 (UP LE), SDO/HMI/NASA; 37 (UP RT), SDO/NASA; 37 (LO LE), SDO/NASA; 38 (UP RT), SDO/NASA; 38 (CTR RT), SDO/NASA; 38 (LO LE), JPL/NASA; 40 (CTR LE), JHU Applied Physics Laboratory/Carnegie Institution of Washington/NASA; 41 (CTR RT), NASA; 41 (LO RT), JHU Applied Physics Laboratory/Carnegie Institution of Washington/NASA; 41 (LO LE), JHU Applied Physics Laboratory/Carnegie Institution of Washington/NASA; 42 (CTR RT), JHU Applied Physics Laboratory/Carnegie Institution of Washington/NASA; 42 (LO LE), NASA; 43 (LO LE), JHU Applied Physics Laboratory/Carnegie Institution of Washington/NASA; 43 (LO RT) European Space Agency, P. Carril/SPL; 44 (UP LE), JPL/NASA; 44 (UP RT), Kenneth Sponsler/SS; 44 (CTR RT), Irina Kuzmina/SS; 44 (LO RT), TAKE 27 LTD/SPL; 45 (UP RT), JPL/USGS/NASA; 47 (UP CTR), JPL/NASA; 47 (CTR RT), E. De Jong et al. (JPL), MIPL, Magellan Team/NASA; 47 (LO LE), NASA; 48 (LO RT), Stocktrek Images/GI; 49 (CTR LE), Jamen Percy/DR; 49 (UP RT), Giovanni Gagliardi/DR; 50 (UP LE), Koh Sze Kiat/DR; 50 (CTR LE), Qliebin/DR; 50 (LO LE), Norman Kuring, NASA's Ocean Color Group, using VIIRS data from the Suomi National Polar-orbiting Partnership/NASA; 51 (UP LE), Szefei/DR; 51 (LO RT), Michal Cermak/DR; 52-53 (CTR), Matthias Kulka/CO UK; 52 (LO RT), Philcold/DR; 53 (UP LE), NASA; 53 (UP RT), NASA; 53 (LO RT), Earth Missions Image Gallery/NASA; 53 (LO LE), KSC/NASA; --54 (UP CTR), Apollo 11 Crew/NASA; 54 (UP RT), JPL-Caltech/NASA; 54 (CTR), NASA; 54 (LO RT), NASA; 55 (UP CTR), David Scott/NASA; 55 (CTR LE), Pratik Panda/DR; 55 (LO LE), NASA; 56 (UP LE), NASA; 56 (UP RT), NASA; 57 (UP RT), GSFC/Arizona State University/NASA; 57 (CTR RT), Goddard/NASA; 58 (UP LE), Ames/Dana Berry/NASA; 58 (UP RT), Goddard/Lunar Reconnaissance Orbiter/NASA; 58 (CTR), Michelle M. Murphy (Wyle Information Systems, LLC)/NASA; 58 (CTR RT), Glenn/NASA; 58 (LO RT), Maocheng/DR; 59 (CTR LE), NASA; 59 (CTR RT), Foster+Partners/ESA; 60 (LO RT), JPL/NASA; 61 (UP RT), JPL-Caltech/University of Arizona/NASA; 61 (CTR RT, DEIMOS), JPL-Caltech/University of Arizona/NASA; 61 (CTR RT, PHOBOS), JPL-Caltech/University of Arizona/NASA; 61 (LO RT), Lowell Georgia/CO UK; 62 (UP LE), JPL/NASA; 62 (CTR LE), JPL/NASA; 63 (UP LE), NASA- JPL-Caltech - digital vers/Science Faction/CO UK; 63 (CTR RT), CO UK; 63 (LO RT), NASA/JPL/Michael Benson/Kinetikon Pictures/CO UK; 64 (UP CTR), JPL-Caltech/MSSS/NASA; 64 (CTR RT), JPL-Caltech/University of Arizona/NASA; 64 (LO RT), JPL-Caltech/University of Arizona/NASA; 65 (CTR RT), CloudsAO/SEArch; 65 (LO RT), JSC/Stanford University/NASA; 66 (CTR LE), JPL/USGS/NASA; 66 (LO CTR), Paul Fleet/DR; 67 (CTR LE), UCLA, B. E. Schmidt and S. C. Radcliffe/NASA; 67 (LO LE), JPL-Caltech/UCAL/MPS/DLR/IDA/NASA; 68 (UP RT), JPL-Caltech/Stanford/NASA; 68 (CTR RT), Digitalpress/DR; 69 (LO LE), Dhprophotog/DR; 69 (LO RT), Ames Research Center/NASA; **Outer Solar System:** 70-71 (Background), Victor Habbick Visions/CO UK; 72 (CTR RT), JPL/NASA; 72 (LO RT), ESA, M. Wong, I. de Pater (UC Berkeley), et al/NASA; 73 (LO CTR), PL-Caltech/SETI Institute/NASA; 74 (UP LE), SPL/CO UK; 74 (UP RT), NASA; 76 (UP RT), JPL-Caltech/NASA; 77 (LO RT), Nikonaft/DR; 78 (LO RT), JPL/Space Science Institute/NASA; 79 (UP LE), JPL-Caltech/SSI/Hampton University/NASA; 79 (CTR RT), JPL/Space Science Institute/NASA; 79 (LO RT), JPL-Caltech/NASA; 80 (LO RT), JPL-CalTech/NASA; 80 (LO LE), C.Carreau/ESA; 81 (CTR LE), JPL/SSI/LPI/NASA; 81 (CTR RT), JPL/USGS/NASA; 82 (UP LE), JPL/University of Colorado/NASA; 82 (CTR RT), JPL/Space Science Institute/NASA; 83 (UP RT), NASA; 83 (CTR), MarcelClemens/SS; 83 (LO CTR), Detlev Van Ravenswaay/SPL/CO UK; 84 (UP LE), JPL/NASA; 84 (UP RT), NASA/SPL; 84 (CTR RT), CARLOS CLARIVAN/SPL; 84 (LO RT), JPL/NASA; 85 (CTR RT), JPL/NASA; 85 (LO CTR), JPL/STScI/NASA; 86 (CTR LE), ESA, and L. Lamy (Observatory of Paris, CNRS, CNES)/NASA; 87 (UP RT), David Parker/SPL/CO UK; 87 (CTR LE), JPL/NASA; 88 (LO LE), NASA/ESA/STSCI/L. Sromovsky & P. Fry, UW-MADISON/SPL; 89 (CTR RT), Mark Garlick/SPL; 89 (LO RT), VLT/ESO/JPL/Paris Observatory/NASA; 90 (LO LE), NASA/Roger Ressmeyer/CO UK; 90 (LO RT), Voyager 2/NASA; 91 (CTR RT), JPL/USGS/NASA; 91 (LO LE), JPL/NASA; 92 (UP), NASA; 92 (LO RT), NASA, ESA, G. Bacon/SPL; 93 (CTR RT), Royal Observatory, Edinburgh/SPL; 93 (CTR LE), JPL/Space Science Institute/NASA; 94 (UP CTR), JHUAPL/SwRI/NASA; 95 (UP RT), Demotix Live News/Demotix/CO UK; 95 (UP LE), Scott Andrews/Science Faction/CO UK; 95 (CTR LE), Demotix Live News/Demotix/CO UK; 96 (LO LE), Mark Garlick/CO UK; 96 (UP RT), R. Hurt (SSC-Caltech)/JPL-Caltech/NASA; 97 (UP RT), Friedrich Saurer/SPL; 98-99 (CTR), Mark Garlick/SPL; 98 (LO LE), JPL-Caltech/UCLA/NASA; 98 (LO RT), JPL-Caltech/NASA; 99 (LO RT), Mark Garlick/SPL; 100 (UP LE), MSFC/MEO/Aaron Kingery/NASA; 100 (CTR RT), Puchan/DR; 101 (UP LE), Jerry Lodriguss/SPL; 101 (LO CTR), European Space Agency/ATG medialab/SPL; 101 (LO RT), Rosetta/MPS for OSIRIS Team MPS/UPD/LAM/IAA/SSO/INTA/UPM/DASP/IDA/ESA; **Our Galaxy and Beyond:** 102-103 (Background), SPL/CO UK; 104 (UP LE), Hubble/NASA; 105 (UP LE), The COBE Project, DIRBE/NASA; 105 (CTR RT), Alex Mit/SS; 106 (LO RT), JPL-Caltech/T. Pyle/NASA; 107 (LO LE), ESO; 107 (LO RT), Ames/JPL-Caltech/NASA; 112 (UP RT), The Hubble Heritage Team (STScI)/NASA; 112 (CTR), STScI/NASA/CO UK; 112-113 (LO), NASA, Dalcanton (University of Washington, USA), B. F. Williams (University of Washington, U.S.A.), L. C. Johnson (University of Washington, U.S.A.), the PHAT team, and R. Gendler/ESA; 112 (LO LE), NASA/Hubble Heritage Team (AURA/STScI)/ESA; 112 (CTR LE), NASA/C. Robert O'Dell (Vanderbilt University)/ESA; 113 (UP RT), X-ray: CXC/RIT/J.Kastner et al./NASA; Optical: STScI/NASA; 114 (UP LE), NASA/G. Brammer/ESA; 114-115 (CTR LO), NASA/JPL-Caltech/CO UK; 114 (LO RT), JPL-Caltech/NASA; 115 (UP LE), Celestial Image Co./SPL; 116 (UP LE), JPL-Caltech/NASA; 116 (LO RT), ESO; 117 (UP RT), Mark Garlick/SPL; 117 (CTR), ESA/Hubble Legacy Archive/NASA - Processing: Stephen Byrne ; 117 (LO RT), Gemini Observatory artwork by Lynette Cook/SPL; 117 (LO LE), JPL-Caltech/Harvard-Smithsonian CfA/NASA; 118 (UP RT), SPL; 118 (LO RT), Msc1974/DR; 118 (LO LE), Detlev Van Ravenswaay/SPL; 119 (UP LE), P. Kervella/ESO; 120 (UP RT), Metallic Citizen/SS; 120-121 (CTR), X-ray: CXC/SAO/NASA; Optical: STScI/NASA; Infrared: JPL-Caltech/Steward/O.Krause et al/NASA; 121 (LO LE), ESA/The Hubble Key Project Team and the High-Z Supernova Search Team/NASA; 121 (CTR RT), ESA/STScI/NASA; 122 (UP LE), Goddard Space Flight Center/NASA; 122 (UP RT), NASA/J. Hester, A. Loll (Arizona State University)/ESA; 123 (UP RT), CXC/SAO/F. Seward et al/NASA; 123 (LO RT), CXC/NGST/NASA; 124 (UP LE), Hubble Legacy Archive/Chart 32 Team, Johannes Schedler/Robert Gendler/SPL; 124 (CTR RT), Russell Croman/SPL; 125 (UP RT), European Southern Observatory/SPL; 125 (LO RT), J. Emerson/Vista/European Southern Observatory/SPL; 127 (UP RT), STScI/NASA/CO UK; 128 (UP RT), ACS Science & Engineering Team, Hubble Space Telescope/NASA; 128 (LO LE), Optical: STScI/NASA; X-ray: NASA/CXC/SAO/NRAO/AUI/NSF/G. Ogrean (Stanford University)/ESA; 128-129 (CTR), Roberto Colombari/Stocktrek Images/CO UK; 129 (UP RT), SPL/CO UK; 129 (CTR RT), JPL-Caltech/NASA; 129 (LO RT), NASA/SPL; 130 (CTR RT), NASA/CXC/IOA/A FABIAN ETAL/SPL; 130-131 (CTR), Mark Garlick/SPL; 130-131 (LO CTR), STScI/NASA/CO UK; 131 (LO RT), M. Markevitch/CXC/CFA/NASA/SPL; **Mapping Space:** 132-133 (Background), Dave Yoder/National Geographic Creative/CO UK; 134 (UP RT), De Agostini Picture Library/GI; 134 (LO LE), ullsteinbild/TopFoto; 134-135 (CTR), NASA/DOE/Fermi Lat Collaboration/SPL; 134-135 (LO CTR), TopFoto ; 134 (UP LE), NASA/WMAP Science Team/SPL; 135 (UP RT), Stapleton/HIP/TopFoto ; 135 (LO RT), Fine Art Images/Heritage Images/TopFoto; 136 (UP LE), Olgavolodina/DR; 136 (LO LE), Eddie Toro/DR ; 137 (UP CTR), Attila Jandi/DR; 137 (CTR RT), Vetergor/DR; 137 (LO RT), Oksanaphoto/DR; 137 (LO LE), Linda Moon/SS; 138 (UP RT), Denys Kornylov/DR; 139 (UP CTR), Tony Rowell/CO UK; 139 (UP RT), Jon Hicks/CO UK; 139 (LO RT), Caltech/MIT/LIGO Lab/SPL; 139 (CTR LE), Detlev Van Ravenswaay/SPL/CO UK; 140 (LO RT), Carlos Clarivan/SPL;141 (UP LE), NASA; 141 (CTR RT), Imaginechina/CO UK; 141 (LO RT), G. Hüdepohl/ESO; 141 (LO LE), ESA - C. Carreau; 142 (UP LE), Elmer Martinez/AFP/GI; 142 (LO LE), Scanrail1/SS; 142 (LO CTR), Dja65/SS; 142 (LO RT), Baloncici/SS; 143 (UP LE), Hill Street Studios/GI; 143 (LO LE), Carlos Fernandez/Moment RF/GI; 144 (UP LE), R. Ian Lloyd/Masterfile/CO UK; 147 (UP CTR), DM7/SS; **Space Fun:** 150 (Background), Tomislav Stajduhar/DR; 151 (Background), Icerock/DR

MAP CREDITS

Place-names: Gazetteer of Planetary Nomenclature, Planetary Geomatics Group of the USGS (United States Geological Survey) Astrogeology Science Center: planetarynames.wr.usgs.gov; IAU (International Astronomical Union): iau.org; NASA (National Aeronautics and Space Administration): www.nasa.gov; **SOLAR SYSTEM** (32–33), Kepler 22 and kepler 22b (107) All images: NASA, JPL (Jet Propulsion Laboratory, California Institute of Technology), Johns Hopkins University Applied Physics Laboratory, Carnegie Institution of Washington; **MERCURY** (42–43) Global Mosaic: MESSENGER (MErcury Surface, Space ENvironment, GEochemistry, and Ranging), NASA, Johns Hopkins University Applied Physics Laboratory, Carnegie Institution of Washington; **VENUS** (46–47) Global Mosaic: Magellan Synthetic Aperature Radar Mosaics, NASA, JPL (Jet Propulsion Laboratory, California Institute of Technology); **EARTH** (50–51) Surface Satellite Mosaic: NASA Blue Marble, NASA's Earth Observatory; Bathymetry: ETOPO1/Amante and Eakins, 2009; **EARTH'S MOON** (56–57): Global Mosaic: Lunar Reconnaisance Orbiter, NASA, Arizona State University; **MARS** (62–63), Global Mosaic: NASA Mars Global Surveyor; National Geographic Society; **JUPITER** (74) Global Mosaic: NASA Cassini Spacecraft, NASA, JPL (Jet Propulsion Laboratory, California Institute of Technology), Space Science Institute; **MOONS OF JUPITER** (75) All Global Mosaics: NASA Galileo Orbiter NASA, JPL (Jet Propulsion Laboratory, California Institute of Technology), University of Arizona; **SATURN AND MOONS OF SATURN** (80–81) All Global Mosaic: NASA Cassini Spacecraft NASA, JPL (Jet Propulsion Laboratory, California Institute of Technology) Space Science Institute; **SATURN'S RINGS** (82) NASA Cassini Spacecraft NASA, JPL (Jet Propulsion Laboratory, California Institute of Technology) Space Science Institute; **URANUS** (86) URANUS' MOONS (86–87) NEPTUNE (90) TRITON (91) Global imagery: NASA Voyager II, NASA, JPL (Jet Propulsion Laboratory, California Institute of Technology); **MILKY WAY** (104–105) Artwork: Ken Eward, National Geographic Society;; **SIGNS OF THE ZODIAC** (144–145) Mapping Specialist, Ltd.

ANSWERS

148–149: Galaxy Quest

150: To Infinity and Beyond

1. c

2. c

3. a

4. d

5. c

6. b

7. a

8. a

9. b

10. Gross but true. (The urine is passed through a recycling system on the station.)

11. c

12. b

151: A Starry Show

1. a

2. b

3. False. We see different constellations from Earth during different times of the year due to Earth's position in its orbit around the sun.

4. True. The constellation called Orion, the Hunter, gets its name from Greek mythology.

5. d

6. b

7. b

8. c

9. d

10. True ... but also false. Stars can only be seen through a clear sky with few or no clouds.

11. b

12. a

13. d

14. a

152–153: Lost in Space

1. G

2. C

3. F

4. B

5. D

6. E

7. A

Since 1888, the National Geographic Society has funded more than 12,000 research, exploration, and preservation projects around the world. The Society receives funds from National Geographic Partners, LLC, funded in part by your purchase. A portion of the proceeds from this book supports this vital work. To learn more, visit www.natgeo.com/info.

For more information, visit nationalgeographic.com, call 1-800-647-5463, or write to the following address:
National Geographic Partners
1145 17th Street N.W.
Washington, D.C. 20036-4688 U.S.A.

Visit us online at nationalgeographic.com/books

For librarians and teachers: ngchildrensbooks.org

More for kids from National Geographic:
kids.nationalgeographic.com

For information about special discounts for bulk purchases, please contact National Geographic Books Special Sales: specialsales@natgeo.com

For rights or permissions inquiries, please contact National Geographic Books Subsidiary Rights: bookrights@natgeo.com

This book was created for National Geographic Partners, LLC, by Bender Richardson White.

The publisher gratefully acknowledges the contributions of the following: astronomy researcher Barry DeCristofano; expert reviewer Andrew Fazekas; photo editors Jeff Heimsath and Sharon Dortenzio; mapmaker Mike McNey; indexer Amron Gravett; project editor Catherine Farley; project managers Lionel Bender, Shira Evans, Priyanka Lamichhane, and Angela Modany; art director Callie Broaddus; designer Ben White; administrator Kim Richardson; illustrators David Aguilar and Stefan Chabluk.

Library of Congress Cataloging-in-Publication Data

Names: National Geographic Society (U.S.)
Title: Ultimate space atlas.
Description: Washington, DC : National Geographic, 2017.
  | Audience: Age 8-12. | Audience: Grade 4 to 6. | Includes bibliographical references and index.
Identifiers: LCCN 2016050201| ISBN 9781426328022 (pbk. : alk. paper) | ISBN 9781426328039 (hardcover : alk. paper)
Subjects: LCSH: Satellite geodesy--Juvenile literature. | Earth (Planet)--Remote-sensing images--Juvenile literature. | Physical geography--Juvenile literature. | Earth sciences--Remote sensing--Juvenile literature.
Classification: LCC QB343 .U48 2017 | DDC 550--dc23
LC record available at https://lccn.loc.gov/2016050201

Printed in Hong Kong
17/THK/1